WHO AM I TO JUDGE

My Life and the Shocking World of Squalor and
Tears on the Streets of the City of Angeles

To. Judy
with my grateful thanks
for your cooperation in
bringing this to the
readers — Nandi.

To Paul,
with my compliments
your friend - Nandi.

WHO AM I TO JUDGE

Copyright © **Teera de Fonseka**

First Edition 2020

ISBN **978-955-43915-3-6**

Published by: **MediTecch Data International, Los Angeles, USA**

The cover design and layout: **Manjula Kumara Gamage, Sri Lanka**

Printed at: **NEO Graphics, Sri Lanka**

WHO AM I TO JUDGE

TEERA DE FONSEKA

A MediTecch Data International Publication

DEDICATION

With love to my family & friends featured within these covers, specially to my friends in part three who make the streets of the city of angeles their home.

***

IT WAS A ROAD LESS TRAVELLED!
BUT IT WAS MY ROAD

"People hasten to judge in order not to be judged themselves."

- Albert Camus -

CONTENTS

WHO AM I TO JUDGE

EDITOR'S PREFACE

It has been five years since the author published *TEERA: A Life of Hope an, Fulfilment.* The riveting autobiography with a gripping narrative of the terrifying journey of her life in her homeland records how she went from one challenging situation to another, each one being more taxing than the one before. It all led her to a life of being at the mercy of a group of nuns, who sheltered her from the danger that was pursuing her, while her children were forced to depend on relatives to care for them. Now she is ready to bring you a sequel narrating her enriching and eventful life since she arrived in the United States and was reunited with her children.

She begins the equally alluring sequel with a synopsis of her arduous life before leaving her native land. A victim of violence from her very young days, she found solace in a caring husband and settled down in a loving home with her two children. That was to be an all too brief an interlude before violence comes with a vengeance to murder her husband and seriously injure her, leaving an indelible reminder across her face of the life of violence she had to endure. It did not end there when the vulnerable Teera became the abused wife of an alcoholic second husband who gave her a third child. Shortly, she was separated from her children and living at the mercy of good Samaritans.

In part two, she recounts her life since fortunes changed, and her long-lost brother sponsored her to immigrate to the United States, and her children who were living with relatives in three different continents, finally joined her. Though the memories of the past never ceased to haunt her, she gradually built a life of contentment, and a slew of rich experiences came her way that is vividly related to us in part two. Perhaps, the most engaging experience of all was the narrating her own fascinating but tragic story that found its way to the bestseller list of Amazon Prime.

Part three of this sequel is the heart of the book and the reason why the reader will find this book to be both enthralling and educational. In this important section, she chronicles her intimate interactions over time with fifteen individuals, who are at home on the street, embracing the hidden culture of homelessness. In this extraordinary part of the book, she has created a moving portrait of a troubled people, in a desperate world few ever see.

They reveal the formidable struggles they face every day, from catastrophic health issues to routine threats of physical and sexual assault. But they also speak about their own intellectual interests and spiritual lives, Illuminating the rich and complicated humanity that surrounds them, which challenges stereotypes about homeless people and provides jarring, unforgettable insights into an exponentially increasing section of society.

She has brought forth her profound experiences with those she introduces to us and presents them with great care and elegant craftsmanship in her own unique style.

What emerges from the stories retold to us by Teera is that it is the result of systemic or societal barriers, a lack of affordable and appropriate housing, the individual's household's financial, mental, cognitive, behavioral, or physical challenges, or racism and discrimination. Most people do not choose to be homeless, and the experience is generally negative, unpleasant, stressful, and distressing. Teera delves into these complex realities of homelessness to paint a gripping picture of individuals living on the street and their daily survival strategies.

Most of all, what they crave is for someone to listen to their stories, and Teera was a ready and patient listener. Listen she did, by person and by phone for hours on end. In many ways, a homeless individual becomes a bystander as his routine takes over his rational thinking, and the burden of finding a solution belongs to those who care for the person concerned. Teera was there in many situations to provide advice and assistance when she saw anyone who needed help or came to her.

Giving the rationale for her narration here, she writes, "There was nothing strange about the homeless strangers that crossed my path unexpectedly. These encounters compel me to write and share in the hope of making a positive difference in the world of homeless".

The narrative of her experiences and that of those she introduces to us in this brilliant, heartbreaking section of the book makes it a part of contemporary history and well worth a read.

The book is written by an author, a profile in courage, whose immense empathy, through her own heartrending experience, is attuned to the intricacies of the physical and emotional damage left behind in the wake of human suffering. The author's own experiences, and that of diverse people she met, are presented to us, capturing their highlights, tears and heartwarming smiles on a canvas in a way that both teaches and entertains us.

I wish to thank Teera for giving me the opportunity of editing her illuminating script. I am grateful to Aditha Dissanayake, award-winning Author Journalist, for as always, reading my work and offering perceptive comments. I must pay my compliments to Manjula Kumara Gamage for his outstanding work in designing the attractive cover and formatting the text for publication. Finally, I wish to express my appreciation to my friend Judith Larsen, the Attorney author, for taking the time to read the text and assuring that it is worthy of publication.

Nandasiri (Nandi) Jasentuliyana
Former Deputy Director General, United Nations

PART ONE

JOURNEY BEGINS

A TERRIFYING JOURNEY THROUGH THE PEARL
OF THE INDIAN OCEAN

༄

"I regret nothing in my life even if my past was full of heart, I still look back and smile. Because it made me who i am today ... Anonymous."

***

Let go of regret. It is nothing more than a scar. You've grown on your path. Accept your past and embrace your journey. You are exactly where you need to be. Relax and breathe. Stay present, understanding that you did the best you could at the time, and you'll do your best in the future. There is no contest to win and no race to finish. Simply love yourself and do your best, and you will avoid self-judgment, self-abuse, and regret.

- Creig Crippen -

LOOKING BACK

—»}·{«—

1

THE STORY THAT CRIED OUT TO BE TOLD

Growing up in the splendor of a beachside paradise Teera's life was arduous from her young days. Eventually, life was beautiful and almost perfect for a while as she settled down with the love of her life, Chandra, and her two gorgeous infants; a two-and-a-half-year-old son named Jude and a one-and-a-half-year-old daughter named Shirlene. In the small community in the new town, far from her coastal hometown, she found contentment in the simplicity of life which provided a warm environment to raise their children. Having grown up in a sheltered home with loving parents, Teera was totally unprepared to face the chaos, turmoil and ugliness created by inhuman cruelty in the world. Her family lovingly referred to her by the nick name 'Bubby' which was an endearing term that stuck with her all her life.

Teera and her husband were employed by the Amparai division of Browns Group of Companies. The family-oriented organization manufactured Massey Ferguson tractors and Triumph Herald cars. They were filled with joy, serenity and a promising future until the night Chandra was violently murdered in the middle of the night while sleeping with his family in peace. The assailant intended to kill Teera, but thankfully she survived because of their co-worker Nissanaka's quick thinking and judgment. Nissanka rushed her to the emergency-room within minutes. A team of doctors gathered immediately to stop the excessive bleeding caused by the injuries, including her severed tongue, hanging only by a vein. In terror, Teera endured excruciating pain as they would not anesthetize her for the fear of losing her life, as there was no time for a blood transfusion.

Over the years Nissanka had become a part of their family. That evening after work, someone pretended to be a friend invited him to a bar and Nissanka was unusually drunk as he stumbled back home reeking of liquor several hours later than usual and apologized for the delay to come home. However amazingly he woke up to the strange noises including a car screeching out in front of the house. Nissanaka kicked the front door opened to see what had happened; he saw Teera standing with her mangled face covered in blood. The sight shook him, but he instantly rushed her to the hospital.

In retrospect Teera is surprised that Nissanka woke up and also didn't panic. Later she found out that their infants sleeping in the same room did not wake up for their midnight feed. They slept continuously through the chaos until about 10 A.M. Obviously, all of them were drugged, including the infants. They were glad to have Nissanka live with them, however gladness turned to gratitude to Teera as she now believes Nissanaka was an Angel of mercy who humbly slept on a folding donkey bed in their front veranda with the loyalty of a watch dog.

Soon Teera learned greed, envy, hate, and jealousy motivated the brutal crime!!!

A distant relative named Somapala married Chandra's sister Sirimathi with the ulterior motive to get his hands-on Chandra's inheritance passed onto him by his father Elias and his brothers. Somapala's brother Gunapala committed the crime but lack of evidence allowed him to get away with murder. On the day of their wedding, two of Somapala's uncles shocked Teera by blaming her when they found out the property was not a part of the dowry. They threatened her, cackled, and walked away to join the ceremony.

Shortly following the murder, Somapala turned the property into his dream tourist resort probably from the money he embezzled while he was employed by the Department of Agriculture. Later, Teera found out that Somapala married Chandra's sister while he was in suspension. Following the investigation, Somapala was fired and ordered to vacate from the Government quarters he was occupying a few days prior to the murder...

Devastated by the loss, and disfigured by a gruesome facial wound, her infants still to care for Teera lethargically carried on an uphill climb, attempting to conquer one step at a time. Teera did not like who she saw in the mirror anymore, which lead to low self-worth lacked self-confidence.

Teera could not fathom the fact that someone wanted them dead. Chandra's mother, Leela, and his sister's reactions after the murder confirmed that they joined the ruthless killers in the belief Teera was the intended target. The conspiracy involved spreading malicious rumours before and after the murder with the intention of shifting the blame on Teera and claimed, it was her fault. They accused others as well and used the blame game to take away the attention from them.

During the time, she met a gentleman who she noticed was different from others. He stood out as a charismatic prestigious young man. It was not that he could see past her scars, but he showed a genuine concern and thoughtfulness that she had not encountered in what seemed like forever. He gave her a sense of security, a blanket of protection as she still feared for her life because the criminals haughtily passed the word that they had not finished the job yet.

At a time of despair and uncertainty, he was her knight in shining armor, who swept her off her feet and saved her from isolation. Most importantly he approached a prominent politician to investigate the murder case resulting in Somapala's arrest. However, after being questioned intensively, he was released without charges being filed against him. In retrospect, now Teera is certain Maxwell's presence in her life kept the killers away from her with the assumption that the C.I.D. arranged a detective/bodyguard to protect her after the investigation. He never left Teera out of sight since she left home in the morning until she walked home after work.

Sadly, the feeling of safety was short lived once he rushed her to marriage. She gave birth to another son.

Maxwell's addiction to alcohol led to new set of problems which put Teera on the edge for quite a while. So, the pattern of pain in her life continued. Amazingly when her long lost oldest brother Sextus who lived in United States suddenly decided to visit the family in Sri Lanka, over 25 years later, he saw her plight. On his return he sponsored Teera and her three children to emigrate to the US following the divorce.

On 17th June 1980 Teera gazed out of the window as the airliner gained the altitude hoping soon she'd have the opportunity to hire the services of Scotland Yard detectives to re-open the 'COLD CASE' to make the criminals accountable for the heinous crime.

However, that did not happen!!!!

Once her children were on their own, Teera had time to think about her haunting past and all those who were kind to her before and after the tragedy. She wrote a letter to her husband's first cousin, Kumara, to thank him for standing strong by her even after the murder. In deep gratitude, Teera wrote a letter to the Welcome House in Sri Lanka as they sheltered and helped her get her life in order during a most difficult time. She experienced first -hand all the wonderful work the Welcome House is doing to help women and children in distress. She and her children got a second chance to be together because of them.

Kumara replied the letter, stating that the people who are occupying the property were doing so by force and had no ownership at all. It was obvious he was worried, as there was nothing, he could do to rectify the situation. Kumara's father refused to sign his share stating he needed more time to think about it at the time Chandra's father and the siblings were signing their inheritance to her husband. Kumara might have misunderstood Teera's intentions believing that she would join him to claim the property. He probably came to that conclusion because Teera wrote to him after 38 years of silence. Teera was flabbergasted shortly when she received a letter from Kumara's wife informing her of Kumara's sudden death. He passed away due to a stomach ailment at 62 years of age.

Incidentally, Teera happened to be in Sri Lanka at the time Kumara's family arranged an almsgiving to pay their respects. She accepted the invitation to join the family and relatives to honor Kumara's life on earth. Teera believes her letter might have given him the courage to speak about the injustice openly which led to his untimely death. The family was in shock of his sudden death as Kumara had no health issues at all

Teera had no intention of visiting Sirimathi or the property, but Kumara's family convinced her to make one last visit on her way back. She had no ill feelings with his sister anymore. When Sirimathi smiled at her it reminded Teera of Chandra's smile and forgiveness became easy.

Shorty following the visit Teera received the news of Sirimathi's sudden death. She was informed that Sirimathi fell in the bathroom, hit her head on the concrete and died. Teera has great difficulty accepting that her death was an accident. She strongly believes it was premeditated murder, particularly considering her brother-in-law Gunapala's violent history and the family's notorious reputation.

When Somapala's uncles threatened Teera during Sirimathi' and Somapala's wedding which took place on the 31st March 1967, they made it clear that the only reason Somapala married her, or in their words, allowed him to marry her", was in the belief and understanding that the property was part of the dowry.

Sadly, Teera could not convince her husband that their lives were in danger.

Teera cannot help thinking that her visit confused the homicidal maniac, and apart from their reputation another suspicious fact was that Sirimathi was only about 4 ft tall. She had never known Sirimathi to be careless, as she moved very slowly and there was no way she got careless at the age of 62. That was not the Sirimathi she knew.

It was clearly visible to Teera the killer had taken control over Sirimathi and her husband. She believes that her unexpected friendly visit rattled the criminal mind leading him to believe that Teera made the visit to make amends with Sirimathi with the intention to claim the property after all these years.

Gunapala's daughter who was adopted by Somapala and Sirimathi was to be married and move to the house. He obviously decided to finish the last of her husband's family! Sirimathi was the last piece of evidence. It now becomes crystal clear to Teera that the crime was committed with the long-term plan of gaining power with the ulterior motive of passing the property on to his progeny. She has no doubt Sirimathi was not given a choice, but to legally adopt the one who presently occupies the beach side property in Dodanduwa. It is not a mystery to Teera at all. The memories of the horror, the pain, and extreme betrayal of that dark night are still alive to Teera.

The pattern of their WAY is crystal clear to Teera. She is convinced they got away with murder again and again.

Teera also received a reply from sister Joan in charge of the Welcome House stating they were having a hard time putting food on the table to those who were there at the time and appreciated her desire to help Welcome House at the time they needed help the most. Since then, Teera raised funds to help keep their doors opened to those who are in great need.

Recently she set up a non-profit organization to help 'hurting children' in need. Please check the website *(www. oceans17hopefoundation.org)*. She is very grateful for the opportunity to give back.

Finally, Teera broke her silence and published her story in *'TEERA: A LIFE OF HOPE AND FULFILLMENT'*. She is now in the process of publishing this sequel.

While the events of the tragic past of Teera's life is fully recounted in her published book was narrated above, in summary, in the third person, she will record the aftermath here in the sequel in the first person.

✳✳✳

PART TWO

JOURNEY CONTINUES

ROLLER COASTER JOURNEY THROUGH
THE CITY OF ANGELES

~

"What made me run away was doubtless not so much the fear of settling down, but of settling down permanently in something ugly".

- Albert Camus -

SETTLING DOWN

—·›‹·—

2

TOWARDS NEW PASTURES

It was my last day in Sri Lanka.

As I refresh my memory, it was not a simple shower! I experienced the newfound PEACE in the POWER OF LOVE and, FORGIVENESS! Believe me it was real! Clouds were gathering that afternoon; the air grew thick and I felt the familiar plop of water droplets on the top of my head. It was a downpour! A clamorous sound of thunder which was quite a spectacle; I slowed my pace and looked up to feel the raindrops beating down on my eyelids. Quietly, I hummed the tune 'Singing in the rain" as my clothes took on the familiar feeling of being soaked and clinging on to me.

Sir Arthur C. Clarke, who made it his home, implied the island of Ceylon is a 'Small Universe'. Recently I heard It was the most ancient place on earth, the wonder of Asia had many names, and will always remain as the Pearl of the Indian Ocean. I fled from the paradise Island, then called Sri Lanka on the 17th June 1980, and arrived at the promised land, which was a reminder of the story in the bible. "God parted the Red sea to his people"

"LORD, YOU HAVE HEARD THE DESIRE OF THE HUMBLE; YOU WILL PREPARE THEIR HEART; YOU WILL CAUSE YOUR EAR TO HEAR." (Psalm 10:17)

I left my country by myself leaving behind my children because I had to. Sometimes the decisions are already made for us. We are courageous and wait till enough is enough. So together with Millions around the world believe in peace over conflict, Love over hate and show kindness to all as we put our lives back together. Let me tell you we grow resilient after every adversity.

God works for the good of those who love him, who have been called according to his purpose. Roman 8;2

When it seemed like a no-way, God made a way. Universe certainly has a way of connecting the dots. I have come to understand when two worlds, physical and spiritual, have been bridged nothing short of miraculous reunion occurs.

On the 5th of December 1976, my long-lost brother came back home during the period I had almost given up hope for a better future for us. I was desperate and was willing to do anything, go anywhere with my children to make a new beginning. Sextus did not even remember my existence as he left home at the age of 17 a few years before I was born. It was truly a divine connection.

My oldest brother, Sextus (Cyril), joined the Royal Navy and travelled the world. He came to the United States in the 1950's, settled down and soon made way for his family. By then they had 5 sons and had a deep desire to have a daughter. The girl they desired was born in the USA. They named their beautiful daughter Desiree.

When he came back home to Sri Lanka after a silence of over 25 years and saw my plight; upon his return to the United States he made way for my family.

I struggled to gather my belongings as one stranger after another brushed past me to secure a place in the security queue, and by the time I made it to the checkpoint I was exhausted

I waited anxiously but knowing START OVER was at the end of the LINE and certain brother who gave me a hand to make it happen was waiting for me.

By the time I got to the front of the line, no one had left yet. All the seats in the waiting area were filled as frustrated travellers who listened anxiously for their names to be called. I uneasily stepped forward, and the officer greeted me with a stony gaze.

"Passport please?' he said in his professional voice.

I gave him my passport and fumbled with my other paperwork. He took a picture of my green card, asked me a few more questions, and again stared at me inquisitively. After a pause he stamped my passport, smiled, and said, "we noticed you getting pushed to the end of the line back there." The officer caught me off guard.

"We didn't like seeing that happen," he said. We didn't think it was fair and you should be the first person to get cleared to leave." The officer laughed with another man he was working with and handed back my passport. The two of them looked back to a window where two more customs agents were grinning and waving. We'll start letting everyone else here leave in a minute".

He paused and smiled 'Welcome to the United States, Ms, Fonseka' the officer said 'Enjoy your new home"

I wanted to pinch myself. I was walking on clouds as I made my way through to the terminal toward the lobby. My brother was waiting with a camera to take my picture.

"There she is!" Cyril exclaimed. The sister that I forgot existed. The only one that managed to come to America, after all these years" His caring words put me at ease instantly.

***

3

PLIGHT OF THE VOICELESS

Four months after I came to the US, I met a friend of my brother's named Liza at the bowling alley. She happened to be one of my brother's bowling buddies. Liza offered me a job helping her at her home to care for mentally disabled men. She was paid to care for them, by the program created by the state of California to aid the helpless.

She said she would pay me $500 a month for the work. My hours would be from 8.a.m. to 8 p.m. 6 days a week. She revealed that she was an immigrant from South America (Peru)and lived in the US for a while with her family.

I noticed she was not abiding by the rules, and it broke my heart to witness the injustice. She fed leftover junk to the patients who were at her mercy and who did not know any better. It was not only the food; the unsanitary conditions they lived in troubled me.

"This is wrong, so wrong," I said to myself! "I see right from wrong, but what can I possibly do to help those who are ostracized as if they are robots." Her absence of compassion and of the sacred program Made me feel uneasy. I wondered how I could help to make a positive difference in those men who were born and raised here.

At the end of the month Liza went back on our original agreement and bluntly said to me that she could pay only $200/-

a month. Her lack of integrity did not surprise me at all. What is new? My brother couldn't believe his friend would change her word, in deep disappointment he told me to quit immediately, but I said to him $200/- a month was better than nothing, and I would quit as soon as I found another job.

Luckily for me I got a break that same weekend found a job offer in Los Angeles. But those men had no choices. Lisa's lack of compassion disturbed me tremendously. Sadly, at that point there was nothing I could do. It was a long time ago, however those faded images came flooding back to me after listening to many stories from strangers, young and old, who crossed my path.

Sometimes one just has to wait for the right opportunity to raise awareness to speak on behalf of those who are 'voiceless' and we have to go back to the past to understand.

**

4
BREAD ON THE TABLE – L.A. MEDICAL CENTRE

On 17th July 1981, I started working for Dr. Walter Jayasinge M.D.MPH. the owner of the Los Angeles Medical center, 679 South Westlake Avenue Los Angeles CA 90057. Shortly, thereafter, I took over the management position of 'Central Supplies Department located on the 7th street in between West lake and Alvarado St. My working hours were 9 am to 7.00 pm. Now as I look back it was quite dark when I left work most days of the year. In recent times, people have asked me, 'was I not afraid to walk down the area by myself.' Come to think of it, it never occurred to me to fear "strangers" I passed in the dark.

Over time, Dr. J became the owner of two high rise buildings on Wilshire West Lake intersection. American and Sri Lankan flags stand tall and strong on top of one building that could be seen from far in all directions in the City of Angels. He made way for many immigrants.

My brother Sextus (Cyril) and Dr. J were good friends. I was told in the 1950s and 60s there were very few Sri Lankans in California. When I was looking for work desperately in L.A. I was told by friends about Dr. Jayasinghe. I met him once when I attended a Sri Lankan function with my brother.

Sarath who had worked for Dr. J previously, lived in the same complex as we did with his wife Mallika and kids. He was certain Dr. J would give me a job opportunity. I got my brother's permission to call him and ended up serving Los Angeles Medical Centre for many years until my retirement.

Dr J had convinced my brother to let him know that I could count on him to be a brother figure since he lived miles away. I stood by his side with the same respect I had for my brothers since then with utmost loyalty. Also, I became an older sister figure to his sisters, an aunt figure to his children.

Though, while taking the flight to the City of Angels to : join the Los Angeles medical center, I said to myself, that soon I might be able to hire Scotland yard detectives to bring the killers to justice, the universe of God had other plans. I moved forward with my life, but still carried a heavy load wanting justice for my husband, for me and my children. It was impossible to move on with my heavy bucket list filled with questions. That fatal night a huge part of me died and many continuous pitfalls broke my spirit again and again. However, the love in my heart stayed strong with God's amazing grace, but the pain continued. I was deeply depressed, and my life seemed completely out of balance.

***

5
A BROTHER'S LOVE

My brother Sextus (Cyril) told me that he was so glad he got to sponsor our immigration. He revealed he felt a higher power had called him to sponsor us, while he took a day off and came to Los Angeles while standing in line to file the papers. His words meant a lot to me from a man that outwardly did not believe in religion. I still hold on to the birthday cards that he sent me in his final years on earth. It read 'You touch others with God's Love." The card with the same words twice last two years in a row. The second one gave me more assurance he really meant every word written by Hallmark.

I was honored more than words can express. God calls us to be servants for his glory rather than for recognition and fame. God's approval is far more satisfying then human praise. I want to be effective far more than to be rich and have an uneasy relationship with wealth. One must believe that 'awaken once to help others and rejoice in their triumphs'

He did not even remember my existence, but saw the plight of his fallen youngest sister, picked me from the pit, sheltered and treated me with kindness and utmost concern. He sent me to school to prepare to work according to the American way, taught me to drive and set me free to reunite my family scattered in three continents.

He was a man of Love, a man of peace, was a man of God indeed. I was privileged to be sponsored by my eldest brother who arrived here in the early nineteen fifties. A sensitive, sentimental man. A loyal American preferred to buy things made in America. Every vehicle he purchased was 'made in America" He was very proud the day he revealed to me that he had paid the maximum contribution to the Social Security system and the contributions were stopped completely by the authorities. A hardworking civil engineer, he followed father's footsteps, and sacrificed for his progeny to enjoy freedom.

According to the statistics he was the second Sri Lankan that arrived in California.

I hear emigrants swam rivers many decades ago in search of a better life and freedom. They made way for their families with hard work and sacrificial love as my brother did. During my daily walks I could not help but notice that most of the immigrants have found ways to make a living. Working hard in togetherness to survive in the land of opportunity. I want to tell people "please don't bargain with small vendors; they do business not to build shopping malls, but to live and feed their family.

My brother kept reminding me of the importance of U.S. citizenship as I kept putting it off. Eventually I filed the necessary documents and received my Citizenship certificate a few weeks after my brother passed away, signed by Ms Doris Meissner in May 1997.

It took several years to notice her signature which is another interesting story I have addressed below which was a "'Blessing in disguise". I want to tell people to keep a journal to connect the dots in numerical order to make sense of the life journey and tell your story to the world when it is the right time.

***

6

GLORIOUS FAMILY REUNION

I saw my life unfolding in a way I never imagined possible. On Valentine's day 1983 our family got reunited after living in separation for too long in three continents. Love move the planets – Aristotle.

1982 and 1983 were both very big years for me. I received word that the visas for my boys had been approved. Since Shirlene was safe with my sister, Sheila in Nigeria, Cyril, my brother, and I figured that we would wait to send for her. That way we could put everything we had towards getting Jude and Damian out of Sri Lanka. We planned their trip under a veil of secrecy. Not even the boys knew that we had bought flights for them. The day of their departure their aunt Margaret simply signed them out of school, told them to pack their things, and drove them to the airport.

Neither of them knew where they were going until they got in the car. Jude and Damian were in America with me the very next day. I still did not believe they were really coming home to me. Even in the morning of their flight, on my way to the airport, I still could not believe it was happening. My eyes filled with tears as I watched Jude and Damian trudge sleepily through the terminal. They looked so much older. Jude had grown into a handsome young man. 17 years old at the time. Damian's limbs were long, his voice in transition, and his face still glowing like it had when he was a little boy; a teenager at 13. He was growing up just like I imagined he would. I ran to grab the two of them and held on for as long as they would let me.

I joyously listened to my boys complain about the long flight as I whisked the two of them to my cramped apartment. Just like my brother Cyril did for me I made them a genuine Sri Lankan meal when they got home from the airport. It was Damian's birthday that day. I made a cake and a few kids who lived in the building joined us. We sang and laughed together like I had always hoped we would. That night I slept with a smile on my face knowing that my two sons were home safe with me.

The next morning, I arose to the blissful sounds of Jude and Damian snoring peacefully in the next room. I quietly sat down at the kitchen table, sipped coffee and basked in freedom. An enormous hole in my soul had been filled, and it seemed as though I was about to burst with happiness. Jude and Damian spent the next few days adjusting themselves to their new home. Damian was upbeat and excited for this new experience, but Jude was not. As the time went by, I came to think Jude might have preferred living with my sister and her husband where he had stability. But they picked Shirlene over him.

He was frustrated that we had to keep him in the dark about his departure; that he never got a chance to say goodbye to his friends. He told me that he was going to save money so that he could fly back to Sri Lanka as soon as possible. I tried to reason with him, but of course being a teenager, he would not listen. Jude did not know it just yet, but it was a blessing having him with us. Damian still needed the influence of his older brother, now more than ever. He needed someone to look up to, someone that would love him and give him solid advice, and Jude was just that. I was so happy that two of them were getting along. I could see my family coming together before my eyes and I thanked God for every minute of it.

I enrolled Damian in school and Jude soon began taking classes at a technical college to become an X-ray technician. In his spare times Jude took part time jobs to help support the family. He was an enormous help to all of us physically, emotionally, and yes financially. I was impressed to see him take on so much responsibility.

With my two boys finally living happily with me, I began to hope and pray that the day I saw Shirlene would be not too far off. That following year on Valentine's day 1983 my prayers were answered in the form of an in-laws expired work visa. My brother in law Tony's contract with Levantis motors Nigeria was over. Sextus (Cyril) was in the process of sponsoring their emigration to the US, In the meantime Tony went back to Sri Lanka to settle affairs back home. Instead of going back to Sri Lanka Sheila wanted to come to California and she was bringing Shirlene with her.

I will never forget seeing my beautiful daughter at the airport as she bounced so carefree towards her family that missed her more than anything else. Shortly, we moved to a spacious apartment in North Hollywood. Jude worked part-time and helped me a little but more importantly he gave me the moral support I desperately needed. It was tough but we managed.

It was an enormously joyful day I got to admit Shirlene to the Ulysses Grant high school. Conveniently the school was walking distance from our apartment. We were grateful to finally have a second chance to be together. Shirlene turned out to be a beautiful charming teenager full of promise.

I approached that Christmas, with a renewed sense of fulfilment, a full house, a good job, and food on the table. I felt accomplished and at peace. It was a feeling that at one time, I did not think was possible. With high spirits, I brought my children to the Medical Center's holiday party. The four of us took the opportunity to celebrate and look back on the events of that tremendous year.

The holiday party culminated in a ceremony, where I was given an award for "Outstanding Contribution" to the Los Angeles Medical Center. The award, for me, was a total surprise. Dr, J, his management staff, and Cyril had all been in on it, and they did a good job of not spoiling the surprise. I did not know what to say, I was thrilled to be given the commendation. Life was good.

***

7
BACK UNDER THE TROPICAL SUN

Life takes its turns!

It was 9 /11/2007. PATRIOT DAY! I was very worried when we got word that my brother Marcus, had fallen ill and the family had given up hope. I had missed my parents' funerals, two of my brother's funerals and could not stand the idea of missing anymore.

As I refresh my memory, my son Damian happened to be planning a trip to Sri Lanka and suggested I join him. He said "Amma, this might be the last time you'd get to see Marcus' uncle alive, I know he means so much to you".

So together we made the trip to Sri Lanka. Upon arrival we were relieved to find Marcus's miraculous recovery. He looked healthy and happy. Even younger than I saw him the previous time.

Long story in brief 3+ decades later I felt compelled to do something to bring closure, and decided that I needed to reach someone that was close to us at that time of our lives, and one person that stood out was my husband's first cousin Kumara. He had warned me about the hate, greed, envy and jealousy of Chandra's mother and sister.

Unsure of his address, I hesitantly sent Kumara a letter thanking him for being there for us and asked for an update of the family. Surprisingly, I heard back from him only a week or so later.

Much has changed since the last time I found myself in Dodanduwa. Most of the family has passed on. Chandra's sister Sirimathi and her husband were living in the beach house. The two have turned the residence into a guesthouse for tourists. Apparently, they were making pretty good living charging inflated prices to pale-skinned visitors that do not know any better.

The sign out front bearing our son's name was thrown in the garbage years ago. Gunapala who we believe was the murderer lives across Kumara's house, and a few houses from my husband's house that was occupied by his sister Sirimathi and her husband Somapala. Some years prior, the two had adopted one of Gunapala's daughters. Gunapala was later elected as a justice of the peace of Dodanduwa and has since been using his power to carry out bloody vendettas throughout town.

I wrote back to Kumara thanking him for his letter. Suddenly he fell ill and passed away before my words had the chance to reach him. That letter I received from Kumara was the last contact I would ever receive from him, and no doubt the last opportunity I would have to attain the closure that I needed.

During the time we were in Sri Lanka Kumara's family was having an almsgiving service, to honour his life on earth, and since we had free time, we accepted the invitation to attend the service that took place on Sept 11th 2007.

Visiting the beach house was an idea brought up by my husband's relatives. They encouraged me to make that visit to the beach house on my way back. I still wonder if that house was worth the life of my husband. We never asked for it in the first place, and if they wished to negotiate peacefully for it, he might have given it to them. There was never any need for bloodshed. That property was never worth ruining our lives over.

I was done being angry with them and for what they had done to us. Letting go of grudges help us move forward light-heartedly. There was nothing I could do to extract from them to erase the pain or bring back my husband. When his sister Sirimathi smiled at me, I saw my husband's smile that made it easier to hug her before leaving. I was ready to FORGIVE!

***

8

TRAGEDY RETURNS IN THE FORM OF DISASTERS

While thereafter, my brother, Cyril, lost everything he owned as a result of going into business with one of his sons. The business failed and he also lost all his life savings, two homes, including the one he was living in Bakersfield. My brother was always witty and full of life, it was sad to see him so beaten down. Thankfully, he found employment at Boyle Engineering corporation in the San Diego office. He moved in with us and commuted to San Diego during the week. I offered him my bedroom, but he insisted on sleeping on the sofa.

Cyril usually sat at the dining table and we talked while I prepared dinner. One day he said to me "Teera I am so glad I sponsored you and your children, today I have a place to stay while I restart my life." He Told me that although his brother Titus with whom he had amazingly genuine bond asked him to sponsor Titus, he thought it was too much of a responsibility and did not do so.

But, because of the situation my children and I were in, he knew it was something he had to do. Although he did not even remember my existence, we were connected during the one and only trip he made to Sr Lanka after 25 years of silence. He recalled how he took a day off from work and drove all the way to Los Angeles and stood in line to file the papers for our immigration. He said he felt like some higher power made him do it. It was so good to have him around and the opportunity to be there at the time he needed the most. While reminiscing about our lives back home, I revealed to him how mamma used to shed tears every New Years' eve looking at the pictures of him and our brother Theobald who died at infancy. I told him I was so glad he made that trip when our parents were still alive.

In a few months Cyril moved out when he was transferred to the office in Bakersfield. I am so glad we had those quality times together. Jude, my son, too got married and moved to Palmdale to stay close to his sister Shirlene. It seemed to me he was impatient to move away. He might have been disappointed in me as my blind faith in people put us through unexpected chaos. "I was disappointed in me" I was willing to move to an apartment with Damian and offered him and his bride the house, but he declined.

I remember once I was mixing the food for our dog, when Damian walked in after a basketball game. He came straight to the kitchen, saw me mixing food in a plate and asked with a big smile "who are you mixing the food for, is it for me or for the dog? Damian was content with whatever the food I served. Jude on the other hand often would go buy fast food. Sometimes he preferred fast food better than the food I cooked.

Damian's friends were in the habit of being in and out of our house and often, and sometimes they were so loud and annoying, but they were good kids. When I noticed a few times one of his friends was staying overnight I got concerned and questioned why, and his reply took me by surprise. The kid's parents got divorced and both parents left town, and he had no place to stay. Damian brought his classmate's friend home and shared his room. Over time his best friend became more of a son figure to me. We continue to keep in touch.

Damian was carefree and easy going. Jude on the other hand quietly stayed in his room listening to music and taking care of the house and the yard and became the man of the house. He gave me the financial and moral support to carry the load. Jude too had to grow up faster than any kid should not have to. Jude made a cup of coffee for me every morning before he left for work. I would call Damian in the evening when I was about to leave work to cook rice for dinner as I was very hungry by the time, I left work at 7 p.m. During the weekend I cooked enough curries to last us for the week. The way I see now my sons had their obsessions and respective levels of maturity by then due to the environments and the atmosphere they grew up in.

The poor choices I made in the past had obviously affected their lives so badly. I moved my children from house to house and was in and out of their lives. During those times I hardly spoke with them because they saw me for a short time and then I was gone. It took a long time for me to realise how confused they were of their mother's lifestyle.

Those who took care of my children, told me not to interfere while they were in their care because they knew what was best for my children. I had no choice, so I went along with them in the belief they were in better hands and in fact they were. No matter how hard I tried to have my life back in order, it was a never-ending battle to keep my head above water with Maxwell my ex-husband stalking me all hours of the day.

It is difficult to see ourselves as others see us. I was surprised by the way my children saw me and described me. They never noticed my scar, they thought I was quite attractive. Their words proved to me the saying 'Beauty is in the eye of the beholder.' They silently watched me connecting with other kids and concluded that I was being good to other people's children, because they were not good enough to be my children. They were too confused and not able to comprehend my attitude or actions, probably because they lived with other people, were separated from each other and were being moved from place to place by their mother, who was more like a social worker.

I was well aware that Social workers did their best to find good homes for the orphans, but couldn't come to terms with my children's understanding that I was more like a social worker than a mother to them, because they were not orphans. However, working on my story over a long period helped me to realize that I didn't always fit the definition of motherhood, as I was not able to do the things other mothers did. Consequently, parenting became more like an assignment to me and I became an emotional wreck when I was by myself. I was often bombarded with pain and fear, while making every possible sacrifice focused on the safety and wellbeing of my children until I could be with them.

No one had any idea what was going on in my world. I did not like who I saw in the mirror. All I saw was a defeated woman with the deep scar more like a black rope covering most of the face. It made me feel very insecure and abnormal. Amazingly, however I had the capacity to smile through the flames of fire when I was with people giving those around me the impression that I was a carefree happy person, not knowing my past and that I cried a river hiding in my small room at the Welcome House where the nuns gave me shelter.

Once Damian was driving me to a function and seemed so proud to be driving with confidence. Suddenly, he turned to me and said 'Amma' I want to go back home to visit Daddy. I believe I could make a positive difference in his life and convince him to stop drinking. Few months later he got the news from his uncle in Australia that his dad passed away. Damian was so broken-hearted when he got the news of his sudden death at a very young age.

Shortly Damian moved to an apartment in LA and found me a beautiful two-bedroom luxury condominium in Burbank as I no longer needed a big house. I got a great deal! I moved to the condo believing it was the perfect place to retire when I was ready and was excited to live in Burbank where everything within walking distance- such as the theatre, mall, the park where I could take my daily walks, all within a few yards of my home. However, I was not able to sell the house as expected. It took almost 10 months more and at the time I was ready to walk away as I was extremely burdened with two house payment and mentioned my idea to Jude and he said 'Amma', don't walk away and spoil your credit score again and came to my rescue and gave me a check to keep up with the payment. He reminded me of the time I paid a very high price for filing bankruptcy to have my suspended driver's licence back, due to the lack of finances to pay for the damages caused to a building which made me learn the hard way that there are no shortcuts but there are always other ways. I was grateful to my son's understanding and kind offer which gave me strength to hold on a little longer. Amazingly within a few days we found a buyer that did not need to spend his money with pure intention to lift the burden off my shoulder.

Since my brother Cyril moved to the new place, he and I had great chats at least once a week, lasting almost an hour. He was in good spirits telling me about his new job which paid well and enabled him to negate most losses he endured a few years ago. Life seemed to be moving well for him until he received the devastating news from his doctor confirming he had bladder cancer.

For many years, since my husband Chandra was gruesomely murdered, I woke up every morning feeling that my heart had dropped down to my stomach. Such pain never goes away. When a loved one departs, the physical and psychological pain can lead to a crippling form of complex grief; To overcome this and learn to embrace the unknown is just impossible and like a horrible nightmare.' My husband, lying in that coffin, looked too good in the picture to be dead. For me he appeared neither alive nor dead. I continued to grieve for him and the denial, depression, non- acceptance continued, and I often cried in silence not knowing why bad things happen to good people. I still could not understand why life is not always fair. This catastrophe, the result of human cruelty, was far too hard to absorb. I grieved for my losses and tried cultivating new relationships and taking care of what I still must help me move forward. It is vital to find things we can control to balance the ongoing ambiguity of life. Often, sadly we want what we had.

Three of my brothers passed away within one year. In April 1997 my brother Cyril lost his battle to cancer. Within three months my brother Anthony passed away. More sad news a few months later, my brother Titus passed away on his birthday in 1998. This rapid succession of deaths in my family got me down and hit me hard. I felt tired of my pitiful existence; anguish and worry robbed my peace again and again. Insomnia took a toll on my physical and mental health. Marathon of a life had taken a heavy toll on me!

Shirlene stopped by at a time I was once again in deep depression. She may have noticed my beaten down look the time she suggested me to write my story. She said she was very confused about my many stories and added that it might make a great movie for the 'Lifetime' channel. So, I got myself a spiral notebook, a pen and sat down by the swimming pool and started writing my 'victim' story.

Yet, it was a halting attempt. I was deeply depressed, and my life seemed completely out of balance. No one could save me from myself! That was until I realized that one of the most beautiful compensations of this life that no man can sincerely try to help another without helping him or herself in divine order!

So, I sat down to continue writing my story the day after the Tsunami hit Sri Lanka in 2004 and never looked back. That Christmas day I knew it was something I had to do.

***

9
CINDERELLA STORY

May years after, the day before my birthday, my daughter Shirlene told me she would be busy on my birthday weekend and treated me for a three-day getaway to San Diego the previous weekend.

The following week, on the 8th of November 2019, my daughter got hit by a car while taking a walk. She was critically injured but survived miraculously. She made every attempt with amazing grace to be independent again and focus on her recovery. The enormity of the breath-taking moments cannot be articulated with words. The strength and courage to make it happen so she could once again take hold of her life, one movement at a time, was immense.

On the 8th, I received the chilling call from my son Jude about the accident. He said the chances of her survival were slim. She was in critical condition. He said they would not allow me to see her.

I was distraught when asked, 'Why so many trials, Lord? Why so many tests? I feared to close my eyes for even a second. I kept calling Jude several times. He said, "Amma stay put, I will pick you up in the morning" While sitting on my bed in deep distress, I looked up and saw the lines written on a framed picture hanging on the wall in front of me.

"I KNOW GOD WON'T GIVE ME ANYTHING I CAN'T HANDLE; I JUST WISH HE DIDN'T TRUST ME SO MUCH" - Mother Teresa.

It was way too much for one woman, especially at my age. Matter of fact at any age. Since that moment I expected to hear positive news. I was still sitting down wide awake when Jude called me early morning with good news. He said there is hope for Shirlene for a full recovery. That is all I needed. HOPE. It was the best birthday present ever, the gift of her life.

Her jaw was broken. Lungs punched. Hips fractured and bleeding from brain damage. The right side was paralyzed. Injuries and bruises all over her fragile body.

Finally, I was given permission to see her. When I walked in, I saw her lying in bed. She seemed asleep—a small bandage on her forehead. I thanked God she survived without any visible scars on her beautiful face. I did not want her to survive and go through the pain I endured for too long.

I said to myself she is resting in the palm of God's hands. She needs the rest. It has been a long road for her. My daughter had to grow up with my very difficult sisters in my absence. The choices were made for us at the time I had hit rock bottom and was homeless. Her compelling, inspirational CINDERELLA STORY must be told with great love. Her patience, resilience, and understanding were a rare gift. She believes her father's great love did not allow his soul to rest in peace and never left her out of his sight.

The day after the tragic accident, she had two strokes, and I was told she was 'WRITTEN OFF' by the doctors. I could not accept their opinion. I would not.

When I visited her three months later, she said to me she does not remember the accident, or the hospital stay. Nothing at all.

It was a great relief to hear her say those words as it was agonizing for me to watch the painful procedures done on her every hour of the day. It was way too much for the broken body.

A book I bought at Crown Bookstore in woodland hills, "Don't Sweat the Small Stuff," which I had passed out to many with love came very useful to me at the time my daughter was in the hospital. Andy at the Crown Bookstore sent me a copy by mail when I asked with the hope of passing it on to the family. However, it became an enormous blessing to me during the difficult times. Fuelled by anxieties, I turned pages on the book. I realized everything else that happened around me was small stuff in comparison to the wellbeing of my daughter. The daily improvements brought joy and hope.

Throughout the ordeal, I learned how strong she had become. She was adamant about releasing us to move on with our lives whatever that meant to us. As time passed by, I realized she gave 90% of herself to her recovery, while all of us together gave 10%.

Shirlene is all about 'live and let live'!!

On the 3rd of March, four months after the accident, I was blessed to hug her tight with tears filled my eyes with great love, joy, and gratitude. A RICH EXPERIENCE! I looked forward to that day. I do not just love her. It is a joy to love her. There is a vastness of knowing she is my daughter.

Almost a month after the accident the moment she smiled for the first time, my son-in-law said to me, Amma, now you have something new to write about." I replied, "Yes Her story." Add to our joy amazingly this year (2020); her birthday happened to fall on Easter Sunday. It is imperative I take this opportunity to set the record straight of her actual date of birth.

I am in the process of writing her compelling, inspirational story. A Cinderella story, but not a fairy tale. The times to remember and times I wish to forget. An exquisite journey to the heart of what makes us human. A story and GLORY of GOD'S LOVE.

***

10
MORE THAN A LOTTERY

On 5ᵗʰ January 2016, I heard Dr. Karlyn's Medical staff discussing the big lottery while preparing me for eye surgery. One of them asked me if I would play the lottery. I said I won the lottery many times in many ways. The words just came out of me.

I was so excited to be cared for by Dr. Karlyn and his medical assistants that morning. Dr. Karlyn and I became friends during my visits, and I was confident I was in good hands. He encouraged me during the time we were publishing the memoir.

Within two weeks, I was so excited to have my eyesight restored. It was great to know I could read and write my heart out with clear eyes. The joy I felt deep down in my soul cannot be replaced by a lottery - the clear vision after 36 years of having to struggle with spectacles.

The perfect gift for the new-born writer. I began to find my freedom through my writing.

Two weeks later, I was waiting to pick up a prescription at the pharmacy when Dr. Karin passed by and asked me with a big smile, "How is Sherlene doing?" I said she is fine and out of curiosity, asked, "How do you know my daughter?" He replied, still smiling, "I read your story." That was the first time that question came up.

Many read the story but overlooked the first line, which was the most crucial line, "I am so thankful to my daughter, Shirlene, for making me write my story."

***

—∘⟫ ⟪∘—

11
SHOWER OF HOPE

On the 4th of August 2010 Patrick stood in my front doorstep with a shining smile of a 16-year-old kid. His first appearance made a lasting impact on me. I asked if I could call him Pat. He agreed. Exactly a month earlier on the 4th of July, I had handed over all the stories I had written up to then to Patrick Meissner.

The first day Patrick spoke to me on the phone, there was a reverent awe! I was impressed by his deep confident voice. It was 17th June 2010. The day I crossed oceans 30 years back looking for solace for me and my children.

Having the miraculous opportunity to enter the land of the free, gave me the courage and ability to tell my side of the story with a kid who was born 7+ years later in San Diego, California. Pat turned out to be a young man with the presence of an older gentleman who seemed to have attained spiritual maturity.

I dutifully wrote one story at a time of some people who crossed my path, with the notion that somehow, I could make a positive difference in those dealing with similar challenges in the world as I had faced. The heart-breaking stories are painstakingly real, though I have changed a few names to protect their identity. Because of them I had the opportunity to promote many community-oriented charities to help the poor to improve their social conditions.

***

12
MESSENGER FROM HEAVEN

I slipped, fell, and broke a bone of my right hand on the 20th December 2012. The bone was broken into eight pieces. It became a very trying season for me. I had an appointment with my doctor on the 7th March 2013 and sat in the doctor's office. I was in a lot of pain and stressed out, when a beautiful girl approached me with a bright smile. Her magnetic friendly personality put me at ease instantly. She said her names' Kate. After a quite interesting conversation the very attractive Kate looked deep into my eyes and said "Teera " breaking a bone is only a turning point in your life, and on hearing about the book I was writing at the time, she added "Teera, if you can trust me, email me the latest draft of your story. I will be happy to give feedback I already self-published a book".

She was a stranger, a messenger from heaven gave me HOPE.

I loved her style, and the uplifting positive energy inspired me to change direction with enormous joy with an attitude of gratitude. Kate gave me more courage than I could articulate in words. That afternoon I came home with great enthusiasm.

The next morning, I woke up early, put a pillow to rest my broken arm and started writing my heart out with a new attitude of gratitude and never stopped since then.

After carefully reading the draft I sent to her, Kate wrote," Teera, 'WOW; What a story? Your story and introduction are perfect together. 'BRAVO" that is all I remember.

Later she pointed out many important matters I had overlooked, which turned out to be an enormous blessing, an eye opener. Kate encouraged and supported Patrick and I throughout the process to move forward with confidence. Power of Love! Shower of hope.

***

13
MIRACULOUS TIMING

Almost five years went by and It was 22nd February 2015. That afternoon after having a meal at Maggiano's restaurant Patrick and I sat in silence. Two people oceans apart broke the barriers, truly bridged the gap to transform and deliver a gruesome mess to a message of love. Relief and calm might have been written all over us for a photographer to capture. It was a moment to celebrate the richness of diversity.

On our way-out Pat gave me a high five with a big smile and said, "Teera we did it." Couple of hours later I received a message from Patrick. The memoir was published by Amazon. Aww! A humbling gratifying, invincible and unexplainable power of God's LOVE. I saw a rainbow through my window and the sun was going down gradually. I breathed easy and fell asleep. I just wanted to do nothing but sleep.

We put a book out there with our names on it. It was a long road to get there.

At least once in our lifetime we shoot so high far beyond which we believe we can achieve , so that when we reach it , the unimaginable joy and fulfilment makes you want to move on with ultimate gratitude knowing we survived for a greater purpose.

"The reflections on a day well spent furnish us with joys more pleasing than ten thousand triumphs"- Thomas a Kempis. It was one of those days!

On the 5th Sept 2015, the management at the Crown Books store organized a gathering to thank several friends who encouraged and supported us through the process. Lila from the IWOS writer's group spoke to Pat after listening to him reading a few words from the memoir. She said 'Patrick it's amazing how you became Teera's voice and the two of you coming up with the good 'READ" would make a great movie.

However shortly after the memoir was published, I had to deal with unexpected lash outs, indifference, hostility from those I least expected it from. I was confused.

Life is not as much fun as a McDonald's commercial. Those words of wisdom were offered by a media junior high student. Isn't that the truth"? Every day is not blue skies and rainbows. Some Days we dance on mountain tops. Other days we are trudging through the valleys.

Unexpected questions from friends and family who read the book took me by surprise. Why's why nots, how comes? I felt suffocated at times having to explain why we skipped the stuff that was not worth mentioning in the memoir.

Patrick reminded me "It's not my fault." His spiritual guidance uplifted me and helped me to move on doing the work I love.

***

14
LETTER FROM THE 'WHITE HOUSE'

In February 2016 I met a young man named Demuth de Silva. A brilliant artist/journalist that who worked for the Sri Lankan Embassy in Washington. I was introduced to him by his wife, a dance teacher Chathuri who worked for Sri Lanka foundation. One morning Damith came to me and said in Sri Lankan style "Anty", call me anytime if you need help when your son's not around." I was very grateful for the kind offer. He became a son figure to me over time.

It was 21st October 2016. I wrote a note on a copy of my memoir to the first Lady Michelle Obama "you made us proud" with the intention of sending it to her prior to their departure from the "White house. I called Damith and expressed my desire and he agreed it was a great idea.

He stopped by at my office, wrapped the book carefully, addressed it neatly to the First lady Michelle Obama and told me to send it express mail as it was almost time for the elections. He also gave me the email address to write a note to her. He was certain she would respond to me. I wrote a few lines to the first lady and added "it's a good read" Damith was excited he got to help me in the process. Few days later I learned that it was Damith's last day at work.

My story book made its way to the "white house. It was such a gratifying experience to receive a "thank you" note from the first lady Michelle Obama within a few days. Martha at the reception got so excited when I showed her the letter from the first lady. She shared the news with everyone passing by with great enthusiasm. I was deeply honoured by her loving gesture.

On the 10th of January 2017 when President Obama delivered his farewell speech, he thanked the first lady with the same words I wrote, "you made us proud." I was so excited to hear him say the same words.

***

15
ON ASSIGNMENT

Four days after the memoir was published, a phone call came from my former boss when I least expected. I was still lying in bed basking in joy as finally the heavy load was lifted off me. It was a mountain top experience! But there was work lined up for me down below. I knew it was my time to get out of my comfort zone as soon as the call came. I was offered an assignment to go to Sri Lanka, which I accepted cheerfully filled with joy to serve with love.

I slept and dreamt that life was a joy, I awoke and saw that life was service; I acted and behold service was joy. (Rabindranath Tagore)

I surrendered with great faith not knowing if I had the capacity to handle the responsibilities. Live in the moments we dare to take. There is no mountain too great when you have a reason to climb.

On 7ᵗʰ March 2015 I walked out of the Katunayake Airport in Sri Lanka pushing a disabled elderly lady in a wheelchair with a copy of my memoir in my handbag. I smiled with all the strangers on the way out as I did when I was a naive gullible child. A young man was waiting at the entrance with a sign held high "TEERA" written with big letters and a driver was waiting with the door opened by a luxury vehicle to take us to our destination.

"Faith is taking the first step even when you don't see the whole staircase". - Martin Luther King.

I did not realize what an amazing and gratifying opportunity it was until after completing the assignment successfully. After a couple of days' rest, I learned it was the perfect time to go back to my homeland and reconnect with a few of my friends and family who supported me through the process of writing my story.

As usual I followed my heart: Pure intentions never go unrewarded. It became a very uplifting divine experience. I reminisce with joy.

During a reunion something unexpected revealed by my former co-workers of Browns Group took me by surprise. I was told they were glad I wrote my side of the story as I was judged wrongly, because of the rumours heard about one of my sisters that was spread maliciously by the criminals , before and after the murder with the intention of shifting the blame on me.

The rumour stated was that it was 'all my fault."

Obviously, they were misled by the criminals and passed on with judgemental criticism.

Looking back in retrospect the rumours spread after my departure were ridiculous. The rumour was that I had lost my mind, left the children high and dry and went to England with another man. The tragedy and the continuous pitfalls might have made me lose my mind, but I never left my children high and dry. However, why do I need credit for raising my children the best possible way I could during the time I lost control of my life.

It is amazing what we can get done if we do not care who gets the credit for an act that deserves to be given credit for.

Rumors are spread by insensitive fools and accepted by idiots. We need to seek the truth and people who have the ability to uplift and keep us motivated to live in peace with one another, not voices that are filled with negative words of discouragement, and doubt, that will disrupt harmonious living.

Sometimes people do not want to hear the truth, because they do not want their illusions destroyed. If our eyes saw souls instead of bodies how different our ideals of beauty would be? Whatever the truth we believe in to be able to feel the pain of another person's struggle, to be able to rejoice in another person's triumph, is what truly makes us human.

'You cannot change how people treat you or what they say about 'U' All you can do is change how you react to it"- Mahatma Gandhi.

I will always cherish Arthur, Kate, and Pat for seeing what needed to be seen with their spiritually mature eyes! I am enormously grateful for God's amazing grace for all the divine connections he's lined up through my life's journey.

***

16

THIRTY – FIVE YEARS LATER

On the 17th June 2015 I moved back to Los Angeles, and it happened to be the day I fled from my homeland 35 years ago.

As I refresh my memory, flashbacks of that horrible night become clearer. I remember my ex- sister-in law shouting and screaming when she saw the two men walking me out. I was confused as to why because she saw my bloody mangled face minutes ago Many decades later looking back in retrospect and re-analysing, it is apparent to me that she was certain I was dead, having passed out on my husband's lifeless body; it might have freaked her out to see the dead woman that was being walked out by Nissanka and Hardy Cramer.

A Meticulously calculated masterplan every step of the way to bury the truth with me backfired. However, the rumors spread by the haters and the criminals to shift the blame on me took the attention away which allowed them to get away with murder again and again.

I was miraculously saved to tell my truth and overwhelmed with joy and delighted in enormous gratitude to my one and only beautiful enormously patient, generous, brilliant daughter 'Shirlene' for suggesting I write my side of the story. Writing my story gave me relief, release, and comfort. It also helped me to rebuild my life and move past the pain. Most importantly writing my story enabled me to learn my own strength and give back the love given to me.

I want to inspire others to tell their tales and experience the joy found in relief.

We can never know who a partner of our journey will be, and when we will lose them, or when they will lose us. A part of the success of our life's journey consists of having good relationships with those who cross our path. This requires patience, sacrifice and doing the best we can with the time available to us. We need to love, forgive, give and endeavour to understand, be thoughtful, generous, and helpful. It is important to do this because when we reach the end of our journey, we can leave lasting memories for those who continue their journey.

Over time, our practices shape our everyday interactions and make room for the needs of those close to us. This friendliness expands outward towards others and saying a hello or offering a smile to strangers becomes an expression of genuine affection. As we mature in this practice, we can even empathize with those we dislike or consider enemies until our concerns reach far beyond our own well-being to include the 'peace' harmony, good will and welfare of all living human beings.

The sublime of compassion builds on friendliness. True empathy means we care rather than take care of other people. In the end we can be responsible for compassionate assistance, respecting other people's life choices.

"My religion is quite simple! My religion is kindness" Dalai Lama.

Accepting other people or circumstances as they are gives us peace. We still do all we can to change things for the better, while practicing letting go of what we cannot control; It is either that or madness!

***

RICH EXPERIENCES!

—❯❯ ❰❰—

17

A PLACE TO CHERISH

The Crown Book store in my neighbourhood, woodland hills closed on the 30th September 2017.

I had the pleasure to meet the humble owner Andy Weiss and his lovely wife on the last day. I stopped by to lend a hand to one of his long-time employees named Octavio. Andy and I knew of each other, but we had never had the opportunity to meet each other. I was so glad they came by when least expected.

Andrew held on to the bookstore at a loss for quite a while to take care of his loyal employees and readers with loving concern.

When Barnes & Noble bookstore closed, I was wishing and hoping to find a bookstore in the area and was amazed when the Crown Book Store moved to the same location. It became my favourite place where I enjoyed spending time. I found joy in volunteering my services whenever the manager Sue needed an extra hand.

I got to meet brilliant writers and learned lessons to pass on by joining the independence Writers of Southern California satellite group meetings held at the store once a month.

Once Sue requested me to help a dog rescue event organized by the store. That afternoon when I stood by the store entrance looking after the little dogs a lady approached me. She came to me with a smile and said, "So you are still standing." I wondered why? She said she saw the poster on the store window and recognized it was my picture. That was Sylva Kelegian. I had no idea who she was until that moment. The author of the book 'GOD SPELLED BACKWARDS". an actress, a friend to those rescuing dogs.

I offered her a copy of my memoir, but she refused. She said she would order from Amazon and give a review after reading it. As promised, she ordered the book, read it and gave a great review and also gave it to a movie producer saying it would make a good movie. Sylva found so many connections to my story with her life.

Patrick and I worked on our drafts at the store peacefully and it became our comfort zone! We made precious memories with friendly staff who made us feel welcome at the store.

I also had the opportunity to buy books for teenagers to read and for their school projects for the fraction of the price of new books. Sue saved me the books I valued, especially the book 'Don't Sweat the Small Stuff' which I passed it on to many.

The book "Writings on the wall" with the subtitle "Peace at the Berlin wall" written by Terry Tillman which I came across on the day the Memoir was published is sitting on my writing desk. I got so excited and bought the book as I read the Berlin wall came down on my birthday, and since then I take my birthday seriously.

It never occurred to me that one day I would get the opportunity to mend a broken heart of an Uber driver named Jesus that I will introduce to you later in the text, was also born on the actual day the Berlin wall came down.

When I was almost done and about to leave the store, I saw the book on the shelf right in front of me, ARTHUR CHRISTMAS. Arthur to the rescue- published by Sterling children's books. At the time I was almost done with my sequel when Arthur came to my aid graciously by accepting the editing. I bought the book for a fraction of the original price to give it to Arthur when time permits.

Crown books store turned out to be one of my favourite places that reminded me of the 'Cheers' comedy sitcom theme song.

"SOMETIMES YOU WANT TO GO WHERE EVERYBODY KNOWS YOUR NAME, AND THEY ARE GLAD YOU CAME."

We made history at the historical bookstore which I called the 'treasure trove'. It certainly was my place for a season for many reasons.

I have been a bookworm and written words are etched upon my bones? What reader would not want to hang around books as much as possible?

On October 21st, 2019 I got the opportunity to join a library in the neighbourhood. Once Again thanks to those who care deeply to share. Beautiful minds inspire others. We must be eternally grateful to the reader philanthropist Andrew Carnegie for free libraries that began to sprout up around the country and around the world.

Books are available to everyone, regardless of income or status. This is true for all of us. The library is, and hopefully always will be a place where we can be free.

***

18
'I HEART' RADIO

When Janet from 'I Heart Radio' asked me for a brief of my story a few days prior to the interview on the 6th of May 2019, I was overwhelmed. That night I went to sleep wondering how I was to come up with a brief in such a short time. Next morning, I woke up remembering the 'summary' Arthur Jayasundera made me write. Arthur was our boss the year tragedy stuck in our lives. He accepted to preedit the follow up on my memoir, and insisted I write a summary from the memoir for him to continue the editing.

During the Radio interview Alexander Perris, Janet Zipper and Gale Glassner interviewed me to broadcast on 'I Heart Radio'. Some of the questions Janet and Gale asked me brought back memories.

Alexander Perris was so happy that the interview went smoothly.

Alex complimented me with a big smile for my response to the questions asked, and said I was a natural. It is easy to be supernatural when given the opportunity to tell my story and one has nothing to hold back!!

After the I Heart Radio interview Alex Perris sang a couple of lines of a song that took my breath away. It certainly was an Aww! His voice reminded me of Andrea Bocelli. I thought he and Takisha, who you will meet later, might be good, singing together Ave Maria! I encouraged little Takisha to practice the "star spangled banner, "Ave Maria" she sang beautifully during the times I spent with her.

***

19

LORD'S PRAYER

In responding to some of the questions asked out of curiosity by Gale and Janet during the 'I HEART' radio interview such as the "Dowry" system in Sri Lanka brought back memories of my father's strong beliefs.

As for prayer, prayer brings us into communion with God, he said. The more our lives are rooted in prayer, the more we sense how wonderful God's grace, purity, majesty, and love offer our lives completely to God's grace. Through prayer God frees us from anxiety, equips us for service, and deepens our faith.

The frequently uttered words by my father linger in my heart! He said, knowledge comes, but wisdom lingers. Perhaps with knowledge comes tolerance, with tolerance peace. Learned the hard way patience is a virtue.

My father who was a man of strong faith believed the resurrection of Jesus was considered a much more significant factor than his birth as a human.

He believed material possessions would not add more value to a woman; for a man to love a woman, and his daughters certainly should not have to go into marriage with a dowry involved, money, jewellery, property. He believed in educating all his children to be bookworm.

My parents constantly reminded us of the benefits of a good education. I remember when my brother Anthony who was an A student started slacking in his studies my parents had no choice but to send him to a Boarding school far away, but close to the place where our brother Marcus lived. Father sold our Grundig radio to raise sufficient funds to pay the fees required.

No man or woman should be treated as property of another or measured by his or her possessions. Recently my long-time good friend Manel made a strong statement on Facebook regarding dowry! 'don't give your daughters to beggars." I could not stop laughing at the perfect line.

I write with gratitude on the knowledge passed on to those who sadly did not have the time, energy, or peace of mind to write them down.

***

20
MOTHER'S DAY

I do not look forward to commercialized celebrations or one day of the year to celebrate motherhood, however it turned out to be an awesome Mother's Day when my son Jude met a long-time friend named Gyhan. They both stopped at a Sri Lankan restaurant to pick up food.

Gyhan laughingly told Jude how he, his brother Hiran, and a few kids who lived in the same building took the liberty to be in and out of my apartment before Jude and Damian arrived. At times they demanded a dollar insisting my carpet needs vacuuming.

One of them found a Christmas tree from the trash and sold it to me for $ 10/-and insisted on putting it up. We all had a good laugh telling stories prior to their arrival. It was good to have them around in the absence of my children. He said to Jude they felt like "I was one of them" as I went along with their demands.

I remembered his parents Mallika and Sarath were very concerned about my wellbeing when I got laid off from my work 3 days after I moved to the building. They advised me on how-to knock-on doors and ask for work.

Gyhan called me that evening and revealed that their parents now live in Las Vegas and offered to drive me there next time when he makes a visit to his parents' house.

However, I did not want to wait any longer. Lately, I had stopped procrastinating as much as possible. I wanted to deliver a copy of the memoir to them personally as soon as possible.

"Don't put off until tomorrow what you can do today" (Benjamin Franklin.)

I mentioned to my new friend Nirangala that I was planning to take a flight to Las Vegas and was excited to take a trip to Vegas. On Memorial weekend we left for Las Vegas with her daughter along with Nihal, a mutual friend.

Mallika and Sarath received us at their home with the famous Sri Lankan hospitality. We had a blast catching up as we had lost touch with each other for over 3 decades, while enjoying the delicious Sri Lankan food cooked and served by them. It was an awesome privilege I had the opportunity to hand over the memoir to them personally.

***

21
THANKSGIVING

The day before Thanksgiving I met Theresa at a gathering. She shared some information about the homeless in Los Angeles. What she said touched a sensitive chord in me and I filed away the information.

I spoke to her about my memoir and revealed to her my fundraising efforts to help those in need in Sri Lanka. She offered to set up a non-profit organization to use my voice to help those in need in the U.S and more.

During the Christmas season I worked diligently on the fund raiser. It was their 17th year. Theresa helped me to update the letter I sent out to collect funds and received a decent amount of money. I was looking for a way to send the money as soon as possible when Keshini came to my aid.

Keshini the director of Public Relations of programming of Sri Lanka Foundation who happened to be a former student of Sr. immaculate? in St. Bridget's convent, the founder of the scholarship program for the prisoners' children. She gladly offered to deliver the funds to Sr. immaculate at Welcome House for she witnessed the humanitarian work done by sr. Immaculate during the time she was the principal at St. Bridget's convent as well.

***

> *On the street I saw a small girl cold and shivering in a thin dress, with little hope of a decent meal. I became angry and said to God, "Why did you permit this ? Why don't you do something about this?" For a while God said nothing. That night he replied quite suddenly. " I CERTAINLY DID DO SOMETHING ABOUT IT. I MADE YOU!"*

WELCOME HOUSE

I don't know how many greeting cards you've ever received from a nun. Especially a nun you've never met. But I am praying you will take a few minutes to read this one. Please !

My name is Sr. Mary John Eudes and I run a shelter for the homeless called Welcome House. I feel exceptionally privileged that God has given me this chance to help these kids. There are so many of them. Believe it or not, in the next year there will be many more kids and young adults who will come to our shelter, desperately in need of food, clean clothes and a safe place to sleep. These kids come to us because they are desperate and have no place else to go.

I am appealing to you to help me look after these kids. A small donation from you could help me continue save these young lives, one at a time. Please help if you can. And may God bless you. You can be assured of our continued prayers and gratitude.

In God's Love

Sister Mary John Eudes
WELCOME HOUSE
133 Ananda Rajakaruna Mawatha
Colombo 10
Sri Lanka

Given overleaf is a letter from Teera de Fonseka, whose travails in life led her to Welcome House. She benefited from the love and care that was showered upon her.

Good Shepherd Sisters,
"Welcome House"
133, Ananda Rajakaruna Mawatha,
Colombo 10. Phone : 691871

Date ....

One person is worth more
than the whole world
SME

We are five Sisters at Welcome House. Sr.Benedist
is the secretary to one of the Bishops, Sr.Nirmala
works outside as an Animator in the Holy Child-
-hood, so the work in the house is done by the
other three, Sr.Josita, Sr.Jean and myself,Sr.John
Anyway the Lord is with us and we manage fine.
As you can imagine I am elderly now, but the Lord
gives all the courage and strength I need.

Thank you Teera for sharing something of your
life with us. Do tell us more about yourself.
It is wonderful that you are working for our
Blessed mother in a special way. She will
certainly be with you in all you do. I remember
this, you were a great sports-woman!
Do keep us in your prayers, we promise to keep
you in ours.
With love from all our Sisters of Welcome House.

Yours sincerely,

Sr M. John Eudes.

22
MEMORABLE CHRISTMAS

By the 24th evening I was exhausted, but uplifted. Shirlene Texted me to ask about my plans for Christmas. I replied, I might attend the evening service at the cathedral of Angels then rest in peace. I made a joke, "why do i have to die to rest in peace." No sooner had I sent the text the phone rang.

It was my friend Nihal. He asked me if I would like to go somewhere to celebrate Christmas. Nirangala would join with her daughter as well. I said to myself, why not. I do not have to do anything, just relax, and accept the offer gladly. I borrowed a backpack from Damian and took off without a care in the world.

We went to San Francisco and had a wonderful time until dawn. However, we were sad we could not attend a Christmas service. Nihal had headed in the wrong direction. When he made a U turn and there it was the church of Our Lady of Grace. We had the opportunity to attend a beautiful service that morning on our way back. Keshinie was on the way to Sri Lanka, and God did not expect me to just work and rest. He sent two good friends to celebrate with me.

***

—⟫⟪—

23
PORTRAITS OF HOPE

6th August 2015- My late brother Sextus's (Cyril) birthday. It has been almost two decades since he went to be with the lord. My son Damian stopped by to let me know there was a big event taking place by the McArthur Lake and that he gave a helping hand to the volunteers decorating the lake in the nearby McArthur Park with colorful spheres.

In the afternoon I took a stroll down the lake and saw the spheres had been blown and gently dropped to the lake by several people. I watched the spectacular colorful display in amazement. Later, I got to give a hand to blow the spheres which turned out to be a very uplifting experience. It was a joy to watch quite a team of volunteers working in unity.

It is amazing how creative people get out of love to make the world a beautiful place. Clever creators can see the bigger picture, the formula for success.

MacArthur lake was being filled with spheres. 10,000 children and adults have helped revitalize MacArthur Park as part of 'Portraits of Hope's latest project. Most of the floating spheres were painted by children who took part in Portraits of Hope creative therapy and civic leadership sessions in schools and hospitals.

It was founded by brothers Ed Massey and Bernie Massey. Portraits of Hope graciously acknowledges the offices of Mayor Garcetti, the Los Angeles Department of recreation and parks, and the role of the Department of cultural affairs in spearheading the extension of the exhibition for thousands more to enjoy.

That weekend I had the privilege to meet the Massey brothers and Ed's beautiful gracious wife, Dawn, working along with the volunteers. We had a very uplifting conversation. Dawn revealed she enjoys making music. She is devoted to her loving family and to make a positive difference in the world.

I sent a copy of my memoir to Dawn. She wrote: "Teera, I couldn't put the book down once I started, but I stopped to cry for you and for your infants in devastation for the grief endured."

*** *** ***

24

SAVE THE SIGN

2nd December 2015 for the first time I took the Amtrak Surfliner to Solana Beach to meet Patrick's parents. It touched my soul deeply to see Pat sitting on a bench and waiting for me when the train arrived at the station. His parents Tim and Mary came to meet us by the amazingly beautiful beach. The three of them came from different destinations to meet me. I was overwhelmed with gratitude for the honor. It turned out to be a very uplifting day.

During the conversation Tim Meissner advised me to write blogs on my website. Since then I never ran out of material to write my heart out. Mostly of my experiences with strangers who crossed my path.

Patrick's mother Mary revealed to me she was so relieved her son finally came back home. She was worried about Pat during the time he worked in Los Angeles while working on the memoir. I remember the first day we met. I asked Pat about his mom. He proudly revealed his mom is a mentor! Recently when I read the 'save the sign' article published in Don's magazine. I could not help smiling at how Mary Meissner bent the rules to support Patrick and his friends on their mission to Save the University of San Diego sign at the Alumni Park at Cathedral Catholic high school.

Tim Meissner has created a very impressive system to keep the oceans clean to eliminate pollution, called "Clean water draining systems". A message for generations to follow.

Robert F, Kennedy said, "Few will have the greatness to change history; but each of us can work to change a small portion of events and the total of those acts will be written in the history of this generation...It is from a number of less diverse acts of courage and belief that human history is thus shaped. Each time a person stands up for an ideal, or acts to improve a lot of others, or strikes out against injustice, it sends forth a tiny ripple of hope, and crossing each other from a million different centers of energy and daring, those ripples build a current which can sweep down the mightiest walls of oppression and resistance."

***

25
GOLDEN VOICE

Shortly after Patrick Meissner was introduced to me another amazing connection took place. I found a Precious Pearl named Takisha at the famous Pearl Island Sri Lankan restaurant in my neighbourhood. That is a beautiful, uplifting story that brought me so much joy and fulfilment. I call her voice "THE VOICE" that is worthy of sharing with the entertainment world. Takisha makes her own music and gives new life to oldies! It has been a privilege and a great joy to discover her and stand by her side.

The Pearl Island restaurant, which I began frequenting reminded me of the 1980s comedy 'Cheers' opening theme song. "Sometimes you want to go where everybody knows your name, and they are glad you came."

Whenever I am there, Takisha sang to me! Her two beautiful sisters, Yulisha and Malisha, sat down to chat with me. They made me feel like I was one of them, young! Parents watch us and serve good, tasty food and drinks generously with a smile. They were grateful for the time I spent encouraging their girls, especially Takisha's singing. It certainly was a pleasure to be around them, time well-spent. Yes, it was!

Takisha sang "Rather be" by Clean Bandits, on the stage for the first time on October 24th, 2014, at the G.C. Studios Woodland Hills California. My heart filled with pure joy when she received a standing ovation from the audience. She came to me with a shining smile and said, "Teera, your presence in the audience gave me the energy to sing, with confidence." I was so glad I managed to make it to the event just in time. After all, in the absence of her parents, because Friday used to be the busiest day of their restaurant, Takisha counted on me to be there for her.

It reminded me of the first day Takisha sang to me. Her rare amazing voice took my breath away. I knew I discovered a star in the making. Little Takisha has big plans to change the world for the better. Her thought expresses what I have learned over the years that you cannot know how to live until you know how to give yourself. As Martin Luther King Jr. said, "Somewhere along the way, we learn that there is nothing greater than doing something for others."

In July 2015, Takisha was supposed to sing during the Sri Lanka day held at Colorado Blvd. She arrived late and was disheartened when informed she was too late to perform.

She came to me humbly and asked, "am I going to sing at all today?" She said, "my friends came to hear me sing." The 15-year-old looked so sad, and my heart melted. I was burdened by the gifted child who was counting on me. I had made many attempts to reach out to the committee to bend the rules and give her a chance to sing a song. I was denied.

I got tired of pleading and was almost ready to give up when my former co-worker Prasanna walked by. He noticed my burdened look and asked, "what's the matter?" he added," you look like a loved one has died."

While walking with him, I poured my heart out in great dismay and explained the situation. Prasanna replied, "Teera if you believe in her so much, don't give up! Ask one more time," and I did.

I approached the new lady Achala, and she bent the rules. I thought Takisha might break down under pressure, but she sang with confidence. She certainly knew her song.

I was so happy to see her shining smile once again. The year after, she sang 'The star-spangled banner" on Sri Lanka day. Two years later, she sang the Sri Lankan National anthem, as well, and finished with a look of triumph with a broad smile filled my eyes with tears of joy. As she came out of the stage, I hugged her. Her family joined me.

This time Prasanna came with a smile and said to the parents," If you have Teera on your side, you have an army behind you. I was amazed to hear him say those words. I am grateful to Achala Weerasinghe, who was the director of cultural affairs of Sri Lanka foundation, for she allowed Takisha to sing that evening.

***

26

MORTAL MEN – IMMORTAL MELODIES

Sri Lankan Artist Chaminda brought tears of joy in my eyes!! On November 12th, 2016.

Charming Chaminda's attitude of gratitude is commendable. I was amazed the day I had the privilege to attend the 'Ron Soya' concert sponsored by Sri Lanka Foundation. It was held in aid of the veteran artists in Asia. It was a blast of the past and a lot more than I could articulate in words that filled my eyes with joy and gratitude to be a part of the audience.

The richness of diversity captured my heart and soul deeply. Awe! What a combination. I do not doubt that the universe lined them up to send a message of love and commitment, most importantly overcoming national and ethnic barriers with the sound of beautiful music. It is said that music is the food of love. They are living proof of that powerful statement of harmony in unity. Without any tensions of their differences in nationality and ethnicity, they chose to embrace each other's culture and music with great love and honor. They certainly are made for each other. Chaminda and Preetysha complement each other perfectly with their amazing voices.

The most breath-taking moment was when Chaminda dedicated the award he received to pay tribute to his late father, Maestro Dharmadasa Walpola. He revealed his father never won an award for his God-given talents and his contribution to society for many decades. Though it has been more than three decades since of Dharmadasa Walpola passed away, people still love the melodies, unforgettable classics, the singing ability and qualities of the humble man of principle that he was.

The youngest son of the legendary Maestro Dharmadasa Walpola and the lady with the golden voice, Latha Walpola, followed in his parent's footsteps. Chaminda Walpola is a remarkable singer, guitarist, music director, keyboardist, programmer, and recording engineer, in fact, a musical genius. He came to the U.S. to learn to play the electric guitar. Still, there was a turning point when he met Preethisha, who became his future wife, who recognized the genuine talent in him. She encouraged Chaminda to study oriental music and digital music technology. He was forced by Preetisha to sing in Hindi. They sing the melodies of each other's languages as if it is their mother tongue.

A match made in Heaven to display the richness of diversity.

***

27
BEACON OF HOPE

My son Damian had been looking for his Citizenship certificate and was certain he left it with me for safe keeping. I searched every box I could think of without any luck. I stopped by at Jude's house when I heard he got laid off from work. When I arrived, he was cleaning the mess in the garage that was left untouched since we moved to that house in 2010.

While cleaning he found a box of papers with my name on it and put it in the trunk of my SUV. He said, "Amma, check out if there are any important documents in it." I brought it back to my apartment, looked at a few papers, and it did not seem there was anything worth looking for, and was about to throw it, when Damian walked in. He said" Amma, don't rush to throw the box. Check out a little more if there are any important documents."

There it was. His citizenship certificates! While looking at it he said to me in a very calm voice, "Amma, it is signed by a Meissner." Yes! Doris Meissner. Wow another Meissner. Out of curiosity, I checked the signature on my citizenship certificate, and it was signed by her as well. Aww! One Meissner signed the Citizenship certificate, and the young Meissner became my voice.

During the Christmas season I mailed a copy of the memoir to Doris Meissner and emailed the following letter.

Dear Ms Meissner,

"Yesterday I mailed you a copy of my autobiography. "TEERA a life of hope and fulfilment. It is great that a Meissner let me into the country and a Meissner helped me write my story. IT IS A GOOD READ" If I do say so myself. We are also in the process of publishing my follow up book 'DIVINE CONNECTIONS' Recently I came across my citizenship certificate and was amazed when I saw your name and signature! I feel that connections are everywhere; we just need to keep an open mind and open heart."

Messages of Love sent many ways! many times!!! Merry Christmas to you. Love, Teera

***

28
HASTA LA VISTA

As I go back into my journals, I noticed that I moved to the little apartment # 17 in Tarzana on June 17th, 2014. The friendly environment was pleasant, but the language barrier made me feel like a fish out of water because most of the tenants living in the complex hardly spoke English. As time passed, people opened up to me. Whenever I passed by her, the Hispanic lady named Gloria frequently stood in front of her door and greeted me with a big smile and said, "' hasta la vista baby" with a friendly smile, as she was attempting to communicate with everybody who passed by her.

One beautiful day, when my granddaughter Jasmine and her boyfriend Cody came to visit, they were having trouble with the parking meter. The security officer in the complex came to our aid. Once they left, I apologized for the inconvenience caused and thanked him for his assistance. I was pleasantly surprised when he said to me a few days later that he saw me walking with my little dog Tigger and wished I had stopped by to speak to him. He answered, my name is James. I replied, "I am Teera."

The young man revealed he was born in Uganda. It took me by surprise when asked, "if I am Sri Lankan with a wide smile. I asked how he knew. He said he worked with some young Sri Lankans a while ago and liked the friendly bunch. I spoke a little about myself and told him that I did my writings at Starbucks a couple of blocks away. He suggested I do my writing in the Coffee Bean Cafe, which was only a hop step and a jump from my place. Since then, I have done my writing at Coffee Bean cafe conveniently. Many who passed by him stopped to speak to friendly spiritually mature young James. He spread God's word with love to many who listened to his uplifting words of wisdom.

James looked like someone I used to know but could not place the face until one day I saw on T.V., a rerun of the movie to "To Sir, with Love," one of my favorite classics. His resemblance to the star actor Sidney Poitier was so close. I could not wait to tell him about it. However, my discovery was not at all new to him.

Once I asked him why he chose that job. He laughingly said it was more of a vacation for him. He went through enormous turbulence in his homeland, and his childhood became very challenging since he lost both parents at a very early age. He was six years old when his loving mother passed away. He was into politics, became a badminton champion in his country and said he has a very compelling inspirational story to share with the world when the time permits.

One afternoon James came to me with a big smile and said he had a dream of me visiting his country, and people in Uganda embraced me with loving joy! Wow! That would be a nice dream I wish would come true. We spent a lot of quality time sharing our thoughts about God's word. I did not feel out of place anymore in the small apartment that lacked comfort. The apartment was much smaller than the first apartment I rented in Hollywood in 1981, but the surroundings were pleasant. Having the opportunity to communicate with James helped me to accept my place with peace of mind.

He has been deeply in love with his girlfriend for the last ten years. He did not care what other people thought about him. He laughingly revealed to me that he and his girlfriend share the same refrigerator but different sections. He is health conscious. In the beginning, he attempted to change her fast-food habits, which created unpleasantness. Over time, he gave up and let her be. None of them try to change the other anymore. Eventually, they certainly seemed to have found a secret to a healthy relationship.

When I received the proof cover of the memoir, I asked for his opinion. He looked at it for a few minutes, paused, looked at me, then said with a smile, "Yes, it's perfect; that's you." Shortly after I moved to Los Angles, James came to buy an autographed copy of the memoir and left with a shining smile. I was deeply honored.

***

—⟫ ⟪—

29

HURTING MOTHERS

On the 21st July 2018, I joined my friend Bel, her husband Stan, their children, and friends to support the hurting mothers and the children of the immigrants who were living in separation from each other. The innocent children do not deserve to wonder why, and what caused the separation. Those in power should focus and do whatever it takes to close the loopholes in the system than making children pay the price for the decisions parents make. There must be a wiser, civilized kinder way to create a healthy balance.

The feeling of being isolated from the only world they know is devastating to the fragile minds, who are at the mercy of the unknown. A different world. Intense emotions of separation anxiety cause deep scars. Few lines of a famous song "Irish eyes "came to my mind.

"There is a tear in your eye! And I am wondering why? For it never should be there at all."

Who could relate to their pain better than our family who had to live in three continents in separation because of the inhuman cruelty of a few self-absorbed lost souls?

Miraculously we had a second chance to reunite, but the anxieties and the confusion caused during separation left deep scars! Deeper than the permanently visible scar on my face.

After we got reunited, I remember the moment my daughter said to me.

"Amma, I wish you fed me coconut and rice and kept me with you." I replied, Shirlene, "I wish it was that easy." I could not hold the tears that filled my eyes. I turned around to hide the fears of losing her again, because of my misunderstood intentions. She could not understand, but the choices were made for us.

During the season I was at rock bottom. It was a very uplifting experience to see caring people who gathered raising their voices on behalf of tormented children who were fearful and unable to express the grief and sorrow of separation.

Families belong together! Children need to be nurtured, they need compassion and understanding. Certainly not punishment. "DIVIDED WE FAIL THE WORLD"

It was while I was in that grey cloud that I was snatched out of it when on 5th april 2018 my precious great grandson aiden was born. I lived to be a great grandmother.

***

30

OCEANS 17 HOPE FOUNDATION

I wanted to make a positive difference in the world! Give glory to the God of the Universe! During my last visit to Sri Lanka a wise man glanced at my Memoir and said to me every one must write a book, plant a tree!

"The one who plants trees, knowingly, he will never sit in their shade, has at least started to understand the meaning of life"- Rabindranath Tagore

I wanted to do something special on my birthday. I believed it was the perfect day to open a bank account for the oceans17 Hope foundation. It has been several weeks since I registered as suggested by my new CPA friend Theresa. I confidently walked to the bank but to my surprise, it was not a piece of cake as I imagined. I was told that more legal documents are required to open the account.

I had collected funds from family and friends to give a helping hand to those in need in Sri Lanka since 1999. It has been simple for the last 17 years. Theresa believed I could do more to help on a larger scale now that I finally got my voice by having told my story.

I was not aware of the complicated requirements. The bank officials spoke to me about money laundering scams! I don't understand those gimmicks. This is all new to me.

I left the bank in deep thought and took the train to the Civic centre station and attended the afternoon service at the Cathedral of Our Lady of Angels. While walking out I decided to change the usual route and turned my direction, passed the Amazon Theatre and walked through the grand park, and while I was walking, I saw a line written on a stone, "Faith is the light that guides us". In that line I saw signs- Affirmation. What I wanted to make happen did not happen, but I saw what I needed to see.

The great church leader Andrew Murray once said "Your heart is your world! And your world is your heart, and this is the place God works in our lives".

The state of California executed the certificate and affixed the Great Seal of the State of California 17th January 2018. OCEANS 17 de Fonseka HOPE foundation.

***

31

FR. TOM ALLENDER

On January 13th, 2018 I flew to San Jose and was deeply honored to see Tom was waiting in his car to pick me up from the airport. While getting in I noticed the walker in the back seat. He was still recovering from cancer surgery and was walking with the help of a walker at the time. He invited me to stay a couple of days as his guest in the Jesuits Retirement Center. Tom described the beauty of the area and the magnificent view. It was the perfect setting to relax, reflect and refuel in peace.

As Tom was still in recovery, I preferred to find my way back to the airport, but he insisted. However once again it turned out to be a blessing in disguise. While driving he revealed he does not read anymore. He did not read the memoir I sent him either. That gave me a hint that he would not read the sequel Divine Connections either and will never know what I wrote about him in the book with ultimate gratitude. Most importantly I got to tell him God spoke to me through him on a day I was in confusion as I had declined a very tempting job opportunity as I realized the offer came with strings attached. I was still in deep thought wondering if I made the right decision as I knew it would take a heavy financial toll on me.

I had parked my car in the garage and was walking into the house when I heard the phone ringing. It was Father Tom Allender. He said he read my story and added "Teera your story is all about

LOVE' I will help you publish it'. At once my anxiety turned to gratitude. I knew I made the right decision by refusing to compromise. When I closed one door, another was opened.

I told him Father Tom I am leaving with new energy. He invited me to attend a retreat in March.

***

32
THE RETREAT (JESUS & MARTHA)

16th March 2018, I arrived at the San Jose airport hoping to take a shuttle to the retreat center in Santa Cruz. However, when I called, I was informed reservations had to be made in advance and had to wait until 5.p.m. for the next shuttle. It was only a few minutes past 12.00 noon. I called an uber. The uber driver Jesus was very disturbed when I got in his car, he said when he took the call he didn't realize he had to take me to Santa Cruz, and the trip was not worth it as he knew there were no passengers coming back to town. He was lashing out as if he wanted to throw me out. I understood his concern. He didn't appear to hear me when I calmly asked if an extra $20/- would help but kept complaining while driving.

I changed the subject and asked him about his personal life, that changed his attitude completely. He revealed he lived together with the love of his life for 5 years. Shortly after they got married, he caught her cheating on him with his cousin. He broken heartedly walked away empty handed to his father's house. His father embraced him lovingly and invited him to live in his home and told Jesus, "Son, once you dumped the trash, you don't look back."

He was still recovering from the shock and financial instability. He went on talking and said something about a birthday party. I interrupted him and asked, "what day is your birthday". He said 9th November. That was the first man I met who had the same birthday as mine. I said wow! That is my birthday. Then I asked, "what year?" He said 1989. This time it was an Awe! That blew me off!!! He was born on the day the Berlin wall came down. OMG. I knew it was a sign from Heaven. I said' wow Jesus, you were born on the day the Berlin wall came down. You are a peacemaker." It was more than one could ask for to mend the broken spirit of this young man who was in great pain.

I was overwhelmingly delighted with pure joy that I had read the book THE WRITINGS ON THE WALL-Peace at the Berlin wall written by Terry Tillman. His attitude turned to gratitude. It certainly was a turning point. He spoke with new energy in Spanish when he received a call from his uncle on our way. He said in English" nice lady" to him and looked at me with a smile. I knew he was referring to me! I smiled.

I did not even realize we had arrived at the retreat center. Jesus was in no hurry to leave. I left the extra $20/- in the car while he graciously carried my bag to the retreat center.

Jesus was very calm and happy when he left.

"Sometimes you will never know the value of a moment until it becomes a memory."

Who would have known the book I glanced at while waiting for Patrick at the Crown bookstore would give me the answer that Jesus needed to move on with Joy? I was excited to read that the Berlin wall came down on my birthday which made me buy the book. It was 22nd February 2015 the day the memoir was published. I was basking in joy when Patrick arrived.

Patrick was late! If he came on time, I would not have looked for a book to read and would have missed the opportunity to inspire Jesus to move on just like his loving father advised him.

However, the moment I entered the room full of all-American ladies sitting in silence, I got me restless. The overwhelming silence made me feel out of place, but I waited in line for registration, wondering how to last three days in the hostile atmosphere. Then a lady sitting close to the line spoke to me. She said her name was Martha. Martha made me feel at ease instantly. She was curious about me and invited me to sit next to her and wait until my turn. I told her about Father Tom and my memoir. I took out the book from my backpack and gave it to her to read. After the paperwork was done, Martha offered to guide me to my room, which happened to be next to hers.

I joined the ladies for dinner, few invited me to their table.

They all came in crowds and I was the only one by myself. It was their 2nd or 3rd time, but my first. In fact, it was the first retreat I attended since I came to the U.S.

The next morning when she came to breakfast, she smiled at me and said she had information to share. She could not put the book down and was amazed to read my name and my sister Margaret's names. She read in the book that my real name is Theodora. Her youngest daughter's name is Theodora and the one older is Margaret just like me and my sister. That evening during supper she revealed that she found more connections as she kept reading.

I met Jesus and Martha on the same day. It reminded me how Martha said to Jesus, Jesus you are late. That day I uplifted Jesus.

Martha put me at ease at the time I was feeling so alone and found out that there is another girl who has my name happened to be her youngest daughter.

That afternoon a lady named Carmen wanted to buy the book. She insisted on paying even though I said it is a gift. In the evening she entered the dining room and called me 'Bubby' with a sweet smile on her face. She said she could not put it down either. So many ladies wanted to buy the book, but I carried only a few to share.

It was good to see Donald Fisher after almost 9 years and I was very glad I got to give him a copy of the memoir. Many years ago, I sent the first draft I wrote to Don. He said his mom read it and told him to keep in touch with me. He was ready to edit it, but Pat had already agreed. I laughed and said to Don do not forget your mother's advice. I bought another book with the title "God Loves an Unmade Bed. Spirituality for the imperfect", written by him and had Don autograph it as well. Fr. Tom and Don were the founders of the Life Journey Ministry, and Fr. Tom said during one sermon that Don is his soul mate.

On 17th March 2018, I wanted to give away the last book before the end of St. Patrick's Day and hoped God may line up someone.

Everyone who attended the retreat left that afternoon. I stayed to avoid travelling at night. I had to go to the office to make reservations for a shuttle for the next morning to go to the airport on time. While walking I stopped by the little Knick knack store and in a minute or so a lady got out of the car and walked in. She said she was curious about the place in the wilderness and I explained it is a retreat center. The way she spoke and looked was familiar. I asked if she is from Sri Lanka. She said "yes". A Sri Lankan lady crossing my path in the wilderness took me by surprise. She said her name is Sandhya. I paused, then said "wait, I have something for you." I rushed to my room and brought her the book.

Upon my return I mailed copies to those who asked for a copy of my memoir.

Jesus himself withdrew (in retirement) in the wilderness. Fr Tom Allender knew I needed to retire in the wilderness when he suggested it. It was long overdue.

About a month or so later Sandhya wrote. 'Teera I was having a lot of issues about my life journey, however after reading yours I realized "my life is a walk in the park in comparison to your life."

I am so grateful my story inspired her to be happy with her present circumstances. We became friends and shared ideas.

I had to break a bone to slow-down and learn everything happens for a reason. If I had made reservations with the shuttle service, I would never have had the opportunity to mend the broken heart of the young uber driver Jesus! However, our conversation made me realize calling an uber to make it back to the airport on time is out of the question. Cell phones do not work in the complex, and I had no choice but to go to the office to make that call and because of that I met Sandhya.

Without a shadow of a doubt it appears to me the God of the Universe is with me every step of the way. It is a reminder that we are never alone through the life journey.

***

PART THREE

JOURNEY TOWARDS AWAKEANING

ROAMING THE CITY OF ANGELS: SEARCHING FOR MEANING IN LIFE

ᔕ

"The best way to fin♦ yourself is to lose yourself in the service of others".

- Mahatma Gandhi -

CONTEMPLATION

—❯❯❮❮—

33
REASONS AND SEASONS

During trying times, I question my existence and wonder. Then something happens to remind me why? I recount the events attended, people met, and places visited with gratitude for the opportunities that allowed the United States such richness!

I remember what once my son Jude said with a smile. Amma, it must be hard being You. I gave a lot of thought to his words and concluded he certainly is absolutely correct. I choose love over hate, and peace over conflict at any given time. I learned at a very early age revenge is a dark road and took the other way. I was very confused not being able to understand the world and most of its people and found it hard to fit in and be myself.

My circumstances made me walk the roads of LA with a backpack at times aimlessly wishing to walk to the end of the earth in search of a place to rest my mind. To unwind! During that time, one of the security officers of the office building named Pedro gave me a book with the title "Your Place in The World". Discovering God's Will for The Life in front of you," written by Michael W Smith and Michael Nolan; It was a wakeup call.

I imagined that the wilderness is always somewhere else; a foreign landscape I actively must enter in the act of being faithful.

Truthfully, the wilderness is always where I am right now, and faith is the courage to stay with it when I would rather wish to be anywhere else.

Upon glancing back on my footsteps, I realized paths are made by walking. Do the best you can until you know better, so you can do better. As the time passed by after doing quite a lot of leg work, I learned that I am a writer doing TIME in LA and doing something every day that reminds myself, "Why the hell am I in this city?"

Jesus spoke! I am the light of the world. Whoever follows me will never walk in darkness but will have the light of life." JOHN 8:12

There were clouds of witnesses to give me the assurance I needed to accept the fact that there is a time and a place for everything and that I am here in the City of Angels for a reason. Something compels a writer to write. It reminded me of the famous actor, Alan Alda's words, his feeling of being kidnapped by a strange force.

"I must be out of my mind," I say to myself at times. At other times I wonder whether "Am I being captured by the force of nature? Lately, my head is like an over packed suitcase with so many issues! Subjects close to my heart that need to be addressed. Robert at Patrick Labels Inc. inspired me to continue writing and when I expressed my intense desire to rush my writings, he shared a story of a writer who stayed up all night writing as he was told it was his last night on earth.

He said to me, "Teera, take breaks in between and keep writing" and added; "that particular writer's writings were appreciated very much, decades later." He intimated that I might end up writing multiple books. Robert and his assistant Ed gladly helps me with my printouts.

***

34
SHADOWS IN THE SUN

During my walks one evening while passing the tunnel that separated the park and the McArthur lake, I stopped to look at the work of graffiti artists. Something new is painted over almost every week. These artists know that their creations were likely to be painted over within a few days or hours; so, they were not looking for immortality, or even a product that could be kept, admired, sold, or envied.

These are prayers, wails, applause, not monuments to human achievements but powerful moments from the human soul.

A woman once said to me those who do graffiti should be put behind bars for at least 10 years. OMG! Jails and mental hospitals are already overcrowded with neglected artists. I did not say anything to her, as I understood she had her mind set. What is the point?

The more we open up to our differences, the more we connect to our divine nature.

(Please check graffiti shield.com to learn history and more about Graffiti artists).

During my walks I could not help but notice that the area was getting congested more and more by the MacArthur lake. The poverty and the extremity of the homeless was heart-breaking, and I wondered why there is so much homelessness. Were they thrown out of foster homes after the funds stopped? Were they discriminated against by society? Do they run away from dysfunctional families to keep the distance from drama and rather be homeless and go hungry for peace of mind? When you read the tales of the strangers, I listened to who crossed my path you would wonder what the difference between distracted insensitive parents and foster parents is. So many questions. Recently I saw a line written on a bus "It's the side effects that got them on the streets."

How many of the homeless are university graduates; gifted, unseen, neglected artists! What is their story? I wonder.

I met several artists that left their homes at a very young age and came to the city of Angels struggling to make their dreams come true with the belief that they got what it takes to be a star in Hollywood. It takes a while for one to learn it is not an easy road. A long way from daydream to reality. The reminder of the line 'MANY ARE CALLED! FEW ARE CHOSEN."

If one has no home to go back to and start over, someone to care for them may be disheartened and end up in skid row after losing the battle. If we do not see them, we are not paying attention to those who have become our invisible neighbours.

I had the courage to tell my story because my caring brother made way for us to come to America. We have been helped and I wondered how I may be of help.

My intent was more powerful than thoughts or words. It did not seem like there was anything I could do to turn things around for the better.

I wished the universe would listen to me and make someone in power pay attention to rectify this awful mess in the area. A part of the place called 'The City of Angels", Make it clean, green, and beautiful!!

So, I wrote my burdened heart out!

When I walk down the lake, I am cautious where I put my foot down on the ground, and afraid to breathe because of the disgusting urine smell among the trash all over.

It's not just litter! Toxic waste.

Exhale? Yes, Inhale? NO

Seems like the place is abandoned but

there is life, the place is full of life. Kids playing in the park, women selling snacks/drinks. No drama!!Peaceful.

The population is growing faster every day as if there is a door open with a welcome sign! I often wonder! Is this going to be a Newtown? The whole area is filled with immigrants! Then again "Who am I to judge?"

"If we judge people, we have no time to love them" (Mother Theresa)

The need to make amends is imperative; extremely urgent. What can I possibly do? How may I be of help?

I emailed Patrick the few lines I wrote wishing and hoping someone would hear me and do whatever it takes to improve the quality of the lives of people and the environment. It had become a practice to email my writings to Patrick and his immediate response to those few lines took me by pleasant surprise.

He wrote, "Teera, this is the best poem you ever wrote!" Wow! I wrote a poem. I said to myself. It was a Monumental moment that overwhelmed me with joy, which reframed my focus. I had no clue there is a poet in me.

The journey of many miles began with that one line "WHO AM I TO JUDGE'

Every journey however long it may be, begins with a single step. Once you do and follow your Heart each step takes you closer to your goal. Do what you Love, Give, give, of yourself!

***

35

HOPE FOUNDATION

November 9th, 2017. That morning while taking a walk by the lake in the McArthur Park I was happy to notice several volunteers contributing to continue the work started by the Portraits of Hope Foundation.

Now people can inhale and exhale freely. Nobody likes litter bugs! However, contamination continues! Somebody has to love the people and its environment. Not one body but so many caring ordinary people making it their call to keep doing something about it. The stumbling stones on the way are enormous, but they keep giving their all with pure intention to make the place clean and green. Their commitment to excellence to the tall task is inspiring.

It was not my choice to be here, and while walking round the lake in the park often I used to ask myself" what am I doing here?" I related my side of the story in a book. It was a hell of a ride. I certainly should be living in a better place, where I could breathe easy and walk free. Relax and do the work lined up from far behind the screen.

I love LA, my heart feels for LA where I feel great vibes, but at this season of my life I ask myself "why am I here". If it is possible for me to do something to affect the lives of those around me and the environment in which they live, may be that's God's way of calling my name.

***

36

EYE – OPENER

Over time I realized my encounters with strangers put together a newsworthy "EYE OPENER." I had it posted on my websites, sent to everyone I could think of including Los Angeles Times, Tom Bagwell at the Covenant House and to the founders of portraits hope.org. in strong faith that they would read and pass the word. Sharing is caring! Care to care about the best way you know how!

"It is not what you gather, but what you scatter that tells what kind of a life you have lived"- Helen Walton.

While I continued writing more encounters with strangers that crossed my path something beautiful happened. Suddenly, a calm tranquil voice started reading my writing to me. I was amazed at the heavenly male voice. I said to myself,'

"I must have done something good" I got to do more. "We certainly got to do more we love to do. One fine day I had a bright idea. I emailed Alex Perris the CEO of Right door studios to have someone do an audio of the 'Eye Opener' article. He read the article and called to tell me I am a genius to have written that article. I replied, "Alex, I am not a genius, but it doesn't take a genius to share my experiences with the strangers who crossed my path."

He texted me," Teera, it's your genius and love for God's people that makes the writings so good." He took it upon himself to audio tape it. I was very excited that he offered to do it himself.

I listened to the audio Alex taped over and over with joy and fulfilment. One day I said to myself, "God saved me and made me cross 13,000 miles over several oceans with a long term plan so I wouldn't look the OTHER WAY from those who need to be seen through this life journey of mine. I am honoured for the privilege and feel blessed beyond imagination."

To God be the glory and let us do our part. His words 'Love for God's people showed me the way.

***

DIVINE CONNECTIONS

—»»《《—

37
HOMELESS IN THE CITY OF ANGELS

It all began on the 20th May 2018. I had to be cautious where I put my foot down and was afraid to breathe because of the disgusting urine odour among the stale trash. On that Sunday in May, I took the subway train, got off at Pershing Square station and walked down the 6th street to join my friend Theresa and her daughter to feed the homeless at a parking lot in Downtown Los Angeles. Theresa is a single mother of 4 young daughters who migrated from the Philippines. Through many years of struggle to provide for her family she educated herself and became a successful CPA.

I offered to give a helping hand without having the slightest idea where I was heading and was appalled by the horrible conditions of the living breathing, homeless surviving on the streets of Los Angeles. I was warned to be careful when I walked down the street where the homeless population is rapidly increasing.

An "eye opener! It seemed like a no man's land, but there is life! But burdened lives.

So close to home yet seemed like a different lost world in the middle of the city. While walking down the long stretch, I had no choice, but to step on the street to avoid the tents and cardboard boxes set up for shelter, and the filth spread all over the sidewalk. It was hard to absorb the horrible circumstances in the middle of the extremely unsanitary polluted atmosphere. Men and women seated on wooden boxes watching people pass by blankly looking. weary and disconnected. I just could not make eye contact with them anymore. I held my breath as long as possible and rushed to join my friend.

It seemed like I was passing through hell on earth." Is this for real?" I uttered in sadness. OMG! Why have you abandoned these people? For goodness sake this is the place called 'The city of Angels!"

I remembered the words written by Etienne de Grellet.

"I shall pass this way once; Any Good that I can do or kindness I can show is to any human being, let me do it now, not defer or neglect it; for I shall not pass this way again."

The need to make amends is imperative; extremely urgent, but what can I possibly do? How may I be of help? While walking down overwhelmingly disturbed, I heard an echo of a voice coming from afar. It was clear! Precise. I kept chanting "don't let my feet quit on me" all the way. The walk was a lot longer than expected. I joined my friend to serve a long line of men and women. Some stopped by to chat. Despite their circumstances, few were cheerful and spoke intelligently. I was pleasantly surprised when an African American Gentleman in line asked me if I am from Sri Lanka which rarely happened since I came to the US. Many do not seem to know there is a beautiful Island called Sri Lanka on the other side of the world, oceans apart. I felt important when he said it out loud.

Several disabled veterans who served the country now on wheelchairs were waiting in line feeling inadequate! Defeated! Dread written all over their faces. Once were heroes in uniforms, now in rags; fallen. They remain hopeless as they have no place to call their home, waiting in line moving lethargically for their turn for handouts! There is something very wrong with this picture. I do not get it. Regardless of who they are; no human being should have to live in such rough conditions anywhere in this world, written off, feeling unworthy. This absolutely does not make sense to me. America is the place of equal opportunity.

I wondered why Americans born and raised here are on the skid row. What is their story? I watched the 2017 May Day rally down Wilshire Blvd in amazement. Thousands protesting for the human rights of the illegal immigrants; raising their voices while singing a few lines of the famous song! "This land is your land; This land is my land, from California to New York Island;" The freedom of speech displayed peacefully but loud and clear. Lately, I hear California might be called the Sanctuary City for immigrants. Many raise their voices to save animals from inhumane cruelty out of deep concern, as they cannot speak for themselves. America went to war in the name of peace to save other countries who cannot fight for themselves.

Such is the American psyche. Raise their voices and agitate for such well deserving causes. Generously fund them and even give their own lives to save others in faraway lands, while many are hungry, thirsty, and homeless in their own backyards without hope of a better life. I wonder about the justification! "Love thy neighbour" is a forgotten line. By the time I got home I was physically and mentally exhausted. I was fatigued. I fell asleep as soon as I plopped myself on the bed. Next morning, I was in a lot of pain. My feet were killing me. I could not move my legs. I said to myself it is time I keep that appointment with the podiatrist I had been postponing for a while.

I could not get them out of my mind. My heart was heavy for the neglected people living in deep despair without hope. The images would not go away. Would these people and places be abandoned for ever?

It is of paramount importance we should endeavour to raise our voices for their human rights. When I bring up the subject, some are sceptical and eager to say they are drug addicts, and "it's all their fault", but the fact that matters is not why a person is in difficulties, but what matters a great deal is how we respond to their needs.

Those struggling with drug addiction need help, certainly not conviction. Obviously, people are misled by rumours spread selfishly and carelessly. I want to ask them, have you walked in their shoes? or asked what triggered them to become addicts? But I do not. What is the point? Who are we to marginalize the fallen human beings who live in harsh reality?

Amazingly, the brief experience that day became a longer story as time passed by.

***

38

FRANK'S LINELESS PALM

A week later, on the 27th May I met a homeless young man in downtown Los Angeles who introduced himself as Frank. That morning on my way to the gym I stopped by at the 'Coffee Bean" cafe to get myself a drink. While waiting I sent Theresa a Text message; "Theresa having the opportunity to serve the homeless and got to talk with some of them makes me feel like my work just began. I turned around and saw a young man sitting down next to me, looking at me with sad eyes!

I said HI! His immediate response took me by surprise. He said, "I was trapped by my parents"! We got into a conversation and I understood his need to talk was urgent and said to myself the gym can wait and invited him to have breakfast with me. He thanked me with a grateful smile and picked up his belongings in a small worn out bag of which I noticed a handle was broken. I wished I had a backpack to offer him while he tucked the bag under his arm. On our way to IHOP he revealed that he is Irish British; born and raised in San Diego, California. I was flabbergasted when he showed me the lineless palm his parents burned when he was 11 years old. The scars remain visible and permanent. My question is, how can anyone be so cruel? I did not ask why. There is no justification for that kind of cruelty.

Jesus said to his disciples "Let the children come to me, do not stop them; for it is to such as these the kingdom of Heaven Belongs (Matthew 19;14)

He made a very clear statement to me to pass on to others and said that "those who hurt children should be drowned with a stone tied round the neck deep down in the sea."

I hope and pray that his parents were put out of circulation, so no other child is tortured by inhuman cruelty.

Frank believes in love! Unity. More of an atheist. I reminded him God is within him. He revealed to me that he had no home to go back to and spent a lot of time in the public library. Unfortunately, he said, "they will not let me sleep there". He sleeps at a homeless shelter. He said he is a comedian, and was looking for work, but it is not that easy. At the beginning he seemed so shy, but soon enough he opened up to me and spoke nonstop intelligently and to the point. Frank seemed to have honest opinions about global affairs of the world and its chaos!

His smile reminded me of the first day I met Patrick, my co-author. I told Frank my idea about a village to be reserved only for artists. Frank said I should write about it.

It broke my heart to see this young man so alone in the City of Angels. An attractive young man with a charming personality. After we had breakfast while walking with me, he playfully threw an empty water bottle in a recycling can, then there was an astonishing change instantly when he heard music. Frank danced to the music infused with rhythm with a broad smile. I saw a few moments of pure joy in his face and revealed how music makes me want to dance. He seemed smart and spontaneous, someone who loved to have fun. I was impressed by this homeless young man focused on finding a recycling can throw the empty bottle with mindfulness.

I make it a habit to ask the birthdays of some of the strangers who randomly cross my path.

I asked Frank for his birthday. He said 13th Sept. I remembered Arthur's birthday also happened to be 13th Sept. I told him Arthur was my former boss who is editing my sequel Divine Connections. Frank said, "it's in good hands." He spoke seriously like an older, wiser gentleman.

What a waste of a brilliant mind among many ignored neglected artists? I said to myself. He laughed on and off!

Suddenly, I remembered the Covenant House in Hollywood. About 22 years ago I began to support them as the place reminded me of the Welcome House in Sri Lanka. A couple of years ago I visited the Covenant House and met Amanda Sattler and Tom Bagwell. Tom gave me a tour around the complex and I was very impressed with the work they do to save the youth from harsh surroundings of life on the streets. I wondered how I could be of help. I wrote a blog and posted on my website, *teeraslifejourney.com* beginning on December 29th, 2016; hoping people may read and support the much-needed cause.

Once I had read a book written by Sister Mary McGrady that was given to me through a security officer named Tom Medina. A note inside the book read,

"Dear Teera, I kind of wish God could write to you this note. I mean, I know you and I have never met, and I desperately need to reach out to you right now. I would love to know what God would say to you to convince you to help the kids in my crisis shelter. He probably would say 'some of my favourite kids in the whole world needs your help, I think he would say, I think you are one person who would want to know about these kids, and help them. God knows, I need your help right now! Last night we packed 1,200 homeless and runaway kids into our shelter, and I will see 1,200 more tonight! Please could you help me feed, and clothe, and care for these kids? Please. The need is urgent.

Thank you for helping if you can.

In God's love,

Sister Mary Rose McGrady.

President of Covenant House."

I gave Frank the address along with a card with my name on it and told him to go see Tom at the Covenant House. I was glad I made a connection with Tom shortly after I moved back to Los Angeles. I was certain that Tom would do something to help this young man even though he is in the borderline: He said he was 24 at the time. They accommodate youth 18 - 24. However, after a few meetings with Tom I concluded he would not turn this young man away. At the time I visited Covenant House it never occurred to me to suggest finding solace at the Covenant House to two young people, Serenity Stuart and Frank Conner who crossed my path.

I hugged Frank before he left and stood by the sidewalk and in sadness watched him walk away with a lackadaisical motion.

Frank was in my mind. He made a mark on me.

That night I had an awful dream, more of a nightmare. When I woke up, I praised God for it was only a dream. And then I remembered that Frank said he could interpret dreams if they had any meaning. I was not sure what he meant but he sounded so serious. The bad dream was so real to me. It is only a reminder Frank was lined up by the God of the Universe. I was glad for the time we spent together to let him know his pain was seen and understood.

I did not realize then, but in return for the little LOVE I showed, I was given a lot more, wisdom, assurance, and strength to carry on by this young homeless artist.

As time went by I wondered if he gave me his real name or if he believed he is another unseen young man like Frank Conner, the brilliant young man in the movie "Catch me if you can." One of my favourite movies where beloved famous actor Tom Hanks saw an unseen brilliant young man, took him under his wings, became a father figure to Frank Conner! He turned his life around and helped him use his talent for a good cause. "With God's love and amazing grace and mercy I believe this young man's scars will turn to stars."

***

39

RICK – CANDLE IN THE WIND

Frank's on and off laugh reminded me of Rick.

Rick Passed away on the 22nd July 2016. He had written a letter to his daughter requesting to be read during the funeral service.

A line that said "Don't cry for me, I am not here anymore. This is only my shell." It was a very beautifully written letter.

The young man's on and off laugh sounded more like a cry to be heard and seen, even sarcasm! A mix. It reminded me of the way Rick used to laugh at times. A genius, who was troubled constantly and who blamed his parents and his wife for his failures!

I met Rick at a writer's group meeting while he was attempting to have the group listen to the article he wrote when he was in high school with the title 'I have a dream' about Martin Luther King JR. That day after the meeting on our way out, I told Rick I like to read the article and I noticed how his face brightened. I gave him my address. Next day I received a bunch of articles he had published over the years.

The first time we met for lunch Rick seemed straight forward! He revealed to me a long list of some of his ailments. Blood pressure, cholesterol, triglycerides, diabetics, depression; That's all I remember.

I got a bright idea after reading some of his very brilliantly written articles.

I told Rick I would love to arrange the articles for him in a binder, and he smiled in gratitude and said thank you.

When I presented the binder during a group meeting Rick smiled. His smile grew bigger when he turned the first page and saw the picture of his daughter sitting on his lap. He turned the pages like a child who found a toy he had been wanting for so long. The writer's group got curious. The binder went round the table.

However, Rick did not want to keep the binder. He said it is for mine to keep. Since that day, Rick was given time to speak and read his articles. He spoke nonstop on historical events and made the writer's group call him a walking encyclopaedia. Recently I was amazed to learn my father had a collection of encyclopaedias which my sister Margaret is holding onto at her house in his honour.

Perhaps they were both unrecognized prophets, due to their uncontrollable rage.

A brief story of Rick's life as written by him and told by me.

His parents attempted to change his direction. They pressured him to find different work, insisting that writing and teaching do not pay bills and dismissed his constant plea since he was about 5 years old. Rick was ignored bluntly which made him anxious and very sad. They destroyed his writings carelessly over and over. Their constant dismissal created depression and emotional stress.

When informed about his girlfriend being pregnant, he said he wanted to do the right thing. He was Jewish but became a Catholic, got married to her according to the catholic church rules and stayed a devoted catholic. He said his wife too constantly pressured him to give up teaching and find work that pays more money.

The pressure made him resistant that built rage and made him react to her with mean, harsh words.

He felt trapped by the marriage because she too made constant attempts to change his direction. Over time he became very bitter and the couple sought professional help. During a session Rick was asked by a therapist who he would choose to hold, his wife or Disney Pokémon.

He said to me without a beat he said Porky with a smirk on his face.

That was the last straw. His pregnant wife left two months after the marriage and filed for divorce and got full custody of their daughter two years later. His irrational behaviour made the court decide he was mentally unstable. His constant blunt comments during the court proceedings made him lose visitation rights as well.

The school district retired him at a very young age.

Since then his daughter grew up in a secret location. When he found out his mother knew of it all along and kept it from him he was distraught and felt betrayed. She financially supported her grandchild continuously. She had no choice but to keep silent because of his untamed tongue. Having to keep the secret from her only son might have torn her apart and I believe was one of the hardest things she had to do.

When she passed away there was a substantial amount of money left for him, but the money didn't make a dent about the betrayal he felt. Money was certainly not the answer to Rick. He needed to be seen, heard, approved, and understood by those who really mattered to him.

He lived in the same apartment for over 40 years but did not make a single friend. He said he was flawed, and he does not have a story worth sharing. He said I could write his story If I wished to and mailed me a bunch of his credentials.

During the time I learned Rick could not handle change and any suggestions of change. It made him feel pressured. He resented that and reacted with harsh words. I made a suggestion for him to change his healthcare provider after listening to his constant complaints for many hours and days regarding his healthcare provider. That got him very upset and he lashed out at me.

Next day he called and revealed to me that he has a condition called Bipolar disorder. It was a teachable lesson for me to listen with love but be careful when making suggestions.

Rick was proud to say he had lunch with the former vice president Joe Biden when he was a student at Syracuse University. He wrote letters to him and showed me the replies he received while he was the Vice president. He seemed to have lost his mind because of the pressure put on him to reframe his mind to take another direction. He often spoke about how much he regretted his parent's actions when they destroyed his writings carelessly revealing that it was just a waste of time. He blamed them for not letting him be who he was. It made him disturbed. His peace of mind was affected tremendously.

Sometimes parents' expectations for children put them on the edge!

He said to me that he hated the new technology and hoped it would blow up. It reminded me of Theodore John Kaczynski also known as the "Unabomber."

Rick did not own a TV, computer, or a cell phone. He owned 3 or 4 radios he told me. He typed articles on his IBM typewriter, and frequently sent handwritten articles to the news media. He wrote around 2000 articles, about 400 got published. David Lazarus from Los Angeles Times published some of his articles. Rick came on TV many times. I watched him appear on the news on channel nine once. He knew how to reach out to the media, but sadly not his own family.

He said he almost died when he met with a tragic accident on the 4th of November 1967 which made him give up driving. Incidentally, it happened to be the same day tragedy struck our family in 1967 the day my husband was brutally murdered, and I almost died. Over time I realized he was in my life for a reason and a season.

Rick passed away exactly 17 months after my memoir was published. He looked forward to edit my sequel 'Divine Connections' Rick called me occasionally. Given the opportunity he spoke non-stop. I listened to him for many hours. He spoke with authority in his deep voice. He had very interesting information to share. He does not give a moment to interrupt. It was like trying to take a sip of water from a fire hose that never shuts up. I think that is a pretty good analogy when you think you have a break. Boom you realize it was a vibrating kind of a task. When I managed a moment to interrupt and say I got to go he'd hang up instantly without another word.

Lesson learned when to give my time and when to walk away. He had many issues. He understood issues. Rick was aware of global affairs. He predicted Donald Trump's presidency. That is a reminder of my father's words. He was burdened when he uttered words of wisdom that the prophet is not without honour except in his own land. He too was burdened as the people who really mattered to him, did not appreciate his gifts, the brilliant architectural designs he created and his wisdom he attempted to pass on constantly.

The pressure, unseen by those who matter to them, can make one lose control of their mind. Words can be a continuous haunting echo of torture for fragile minds.

When one feels pressured to change direction it can cause devastation, eventually love turns to hate. I believe some people love and hate passionately. A person should be given the freedom to choose their direction which I believe is the most important decision in one's life.

He was tremendously disturbed and lived his adult life in isolation.

Memories of Rick kept coming to me. He believed my story was worthy of sharing and encouraged me to go see a documentary about a writer who wrote her heart out, which was the only one that got published. Seeing that documentary made me feel very good about sharing my story and the stories of strangers who cross my path.

It is not what happens to us that separates failure from success, it is how one perceives and what we do about it. Rick came from a privileged family but felt like a failure. Having rich parents does not protect one from failure. He attended Syracuse University and later became a part time teacher there. His parents continued to be dismissible. It was very disturbing to Rick that they never recognized his God-given gift. Over time the frustration, anger, and rage bottled inside affected his mental health. His reactions to certain people became rude and obnoxious.

He offered to copy edit my memoir but was impatient with Patrick saying he was too young and too slow and told me over and over he would never finish it. To prove his speed he childishly copy- edited it in 8 hrs once the manuscript was sent to him.

Then again, he admitted he could not do what Patrick did and admired Patrick's abilities, but envied Patrick as he was seen and appreciated. It was understandable. Rick was excited to tell me he found his call by copy editing my story. Since then he edited many stories for free and found joy in having the opportunity to use his gift and make a difference.

Rick was ready when God called his name. He was broken-hearted when his good friend John passed away. Rick liked the way John lived and died. He wanted to die the same way and his wish came true. Rick edited six of John's novels which he had written for several years but held back. Rick gave the confidence and support John needed to publish them shortly before John passed away in peace. They became good friends during this time. Rick often told me that he really missed his company as John was a very sincere humble soul with a heart of gold.

Few took advantage of this complex man's absolute need to use his knowledge generously. Rick was no fool, but he did not care.

I put a lot of love of labour to organize his writings and did not want it to go to waste in my absence. I sincerely believed someday his daughter might appreciate her father's writing. I asked him to show it to his daughter, but he adamantly refused. I could not let it go. So, I got a bright idea and asked him to give me his daughter's address. I told him I want to mail her a copy of my memoir to her. Next day I received a card from Rick with her address and phone number.

I mailed her a copy of the memoir as promised. She was curious as to why I wanted to get in touch with her and asked her dad. After he passed away, she told me, he said to her most likely I was planning to pass on the binder to her, but he told her he didn't think it matters.

During the next meeting Rick gave me the Poets & Writers March/April Magazine. I remember that day an egotistic young man dumped a box full of papers in front of him to edit and rushed out in a hurry.

His arrogance was disturbing to all of us, not just Rick. When I was about to leave after the group meeting was over, I saw Rick looking out of the window. I remember the faraway look on his face while I said bye to him and left. I was very sad about his sudden death, but not surprised at all. I remembered that defeated look.

Rick once revealed to me a Hollywood producer stole his father's story 'Bigger than Life' and changed it to fit in the entertainment world. That got me concerned about my story. I brought it up to Patrick. He took the responsibility upon himself to protect the story.

Rick was very concerned about those diagnosed with Alzheimer's disease. He was very disturbed when he heard a suggestion to send all the patients to a faraway isolated village. He believed they should be given the freedom to live and die with dignity. He spoke frequently about it passionately and used President Reagan as an example; and how the president did not know who he was once he got Alzheimer.

I am with Rick on that issue and hope I will have the opportunity to enlighten others on the very important point he made.

As far as I am concerned Rick's story should be told, as it might change the world of many brilliant artists who would be seen with clear eyes for the gift they are born with and let them be given the freedom to follow their path lined up for them.

The time I received the call about Rick's sudden death I was in the process of writing an article about another writer named Victoria I met at the cathedral of our lady of Angeles. On the 15th July on Sri Lanka day she surprised me by coming to Pasadena looking for me. I heard her calling my name." Where is Teera? Where is Teera?" She saw my poster on the sidewalk and came looking for me. She was the highlight of my day. I asked her why I had not seen her at the cathedral? She replied with a smile "I got kicked out."

I was so glad I asked Rick to connect me with his daughter. She called me that afternoon to let me know the funeral arrangements. I remembered how he once sang to me like a little child. His voice was deep, so I suggested a song for him to sing. I wrote a few lines of the song "Love Letters in the sand" sung by Pat Boone and mailed him. A few days later he called me and asked, "would you like to listen to a song?" I said yes. He sang the lines I wrote to him. I was so glad I had the opportunity to bring out the child in Rick even for a few moments. If you have the power to make someone happy, do it, which might make a positive impact in their life to know someone truly cares.

It might have been the last opportunity to hand over the binder to his daughter. Damian rearranged it in an authentic binder he owned and put Rick's high school picture on the cover of the binder and the picture of his daughter sitting on his lap on the front page. He suggested I take it to Gary Wolin who owns the historical McManus & Morgan Inc. by the MacArthur Lake. Gary picked a beautiful paper suited for the occasion and wrapped it very carefully, even though we knew the wrapping would be torn apart the moment it is handed to his daughter.

It was my God-given privilege to hand over the binder to his amazingly beautiful, friendly daughter. She excitedly accepted it with ultimate gratitude.

I am not a public speaker as I have an audience phobia. I remember the first time I got onto a stage to give a speech about the 'British Museum' I was chosen by my elocution teacher as I knew the whole page by heart and never missed a word during the rehearsals. After a couple of words, I froze and that was the end of my public speaking on a stage. The fear of judgment kept me behind the stage. However, I had to speak on behalf of Rick. As far as I was concerned it was a must. I spent more time listening to him, more than anyone I knew. So, I spoke during the service and sang a few lines of the song I made Rick sing like a happy child. With or without a record Rick made a mark on me.

**

40

VICTORIA – COFFEE – MATES

Going back to Victoria you met in the previous section, who I believe I had met about a year before then.

The first time we met she was shouting and accusing me of judging her, took me by surprise. At the time I was minding my business sitting down by the cafeteria and was just reading a book.

In confusion I said I 'would move" to another spot if my presence bothers her. She calmed down and said, 'no stay' and sat next to me and asked what I was reading. I said Alan Alda! She became very friendly and said she likes him a lot too.

She revealed to me her love of writing. While leaving to get myself a coffee from the cafeteria I asked if she would like a coffee? She seemed so surprised and said! "Really! "I said yes. I bought us two cups, she put the coffee in a big mug, and went back to the cafe for a refill. Then I noticed her stack including a blanket. I realized she was homeless. She was a very neatly dressed attractive woman. I could not understand why she kept accusing me of judging her saying I said she slept with Christopher.

When I defended myself, she said "there is no one else here! You are the only one! It is you". In confusion I excused myself and left. Occasionally I met her by the Cathedral, and we talked about books and her love of writing. I told her to start writing!

Write anything! Then out of the blue she would say I judged her, later I was told she was suffering from the condition called schizophrenia that made her hear voices. I do not know her story but wonder what caused her mental illness and why she got homeless. The last time I saw her was the day she came to Pasadena on Sri Lanka day on the 15th July 2016.

***

41
DERRIS – ATTITUDE OF GRATITUDE

My former boss at Browns in Sri Lanka Arthur Jayasundera who was ready to pre-edit a sequel to my book, emailed me insisting I complete the summary from my memoir, for him to edit it. I was encouraged when given a deadline to get it done to his satisfaction.

I am so grateful to this day that Arthur did not get carried away with the rumours spread to ruin me, in the aftermath of the most trying time of my life following the gruesome incident that took my husband's life and left both indelible physical and emotional scars I had to endure throughout my life. All you need is one true witness to stand firm by you and he was there steadfastly.

I worked diligently on the summary for quite a while, however that morning I was overwhelmed in doubt if I had covered all the areas to paint a clear picture, for those who haven't got their hands on my memoir.

I said to myself, enough is enough! it is time to take a break for a few days. However, I made a printout, put it in my backpack and left the office unsure of where I should go to unwind. On the way I remembered Samuel who I met the day before. I was hoping to motivate him to share his compelling story with Oprah. I took a walk by the MacArthur lake to check if he would be there by chance, but he was not.

Now a days I try not to put off the things I could do today for tomorrow if possible.

I decided to check on him later and walked to the subway station still unsure where I wanted to be. By the time I got on the train I knew the beach would be the perfect place. Lately, I have experienced it was an awesome place to connect with the force of nature's harmony when troubled by uncertainty. I got on the expo train to Santa Monica, walked past the pier, put my shoes in my backpack loving the feel of sand, took a stroll by the beach at a slow pace soaking my feet in cold soothing water. I inhaled the sea breeze with a feeling of peace and tranquillity and loved every moment in gratitude for the opportunity to spend time by the ocean.

I stopped by the Bloomingdales mall as it was getting quite warm and walked into a fast food restaurant to get myself a snack with the intention of sitting down at a quiet corner for a few minutes. While I was waiting in line suddenly the young gentleman who stood in front of me turned around and asked what I was planning to order; we both looked at the board above the counter, I replied ' I would get myself a small fries and a cup of water'.

He revealed he does not eat unhealthy food and showed me the special on the menu. A good meal for a reasonable price. After a pause, I told him it looks good, but I am not that hungry, but I will try it if he likes to share with me. He agreed, and said, but he couldn't sit inside and eat , as he had his dog tied to a tree outside the restaurant, and added that he got homeless many times because he was not willing to part with his companion Phoenix.

I turned around and saw the cute little Phoenix looking in our direction waiting anxiously for his best buddy to come get him. Their love for each other touched my soul deeply. The waiter served us the meal and kindly showed us to a corner where we could sit with Phoenix.

Long story in brief, he said his name is Derris Nile, and revealed to me he is a dancer, actor, singer, and songwriter. He is looking forward to being a producer soon. While sharing the meal he told me he wrote his heart out in 20 plus songs he wrote. He said he does not like to write. However, he said. he wrote a book with the title 'ATTITUDE OF GRATITUDE' I told him my name is Teera, and I had my memoir published

I was very impressed with this homeless young man and knew at once he would be the perfect person to give me feedback on the summary I put together.

Instantly I pulled it out from my bag and handed it to him. He kept reading it continuously without a blink. I watched him quietly for a while then interrupted "your food is getting cold." He raised his head and said, "this is so captivating I cannot take my eyes off it; I cannot put it down." When he finished Derris looked straight into my eyes and said, "Teera, I have written many scripts, and read many more, but I never came across one like this that captured my attention." I was overjoyed to hear him say those words of encouragement.

Then he added "Teera looking at you, it is impossible to say you have gone through so much. You are smiling." Suddenly his attitude changed. He said in a deep voice, "I am waiting to hear from a lady who I am hoping to rent a place to live with Phoenix." No sooner had he finished the sentence he got the call he was waiting for. I was so glad to see his face brighten up with a smile and I was so happy for both when he said to me that the lady, he referred to was willing to rent the apartment. The relief was written all over him. Derris said he was so exhausted from having to move his luggage and Phoenix from place to place as they were homeless and slept in an abandoned house. He trusted me to watch Phoenix and his luggage while he went to the restroom to clean up.

Within about two hours Derris revealed to me few of his compelling stories. A burdened artist; struggling in the City of Angels following his dream. He ran away from a dysfunctional abusive family at the age of 17. Derris Nile wanted to share his story with the world but must wait until it is the right time. He seemed so sincere. We took the same train back with new energy. I was feeling so at Peace by the time I got off the train.

I am so grateful for our uplifting encounter. Derris smiled big and said' it seems like forever since he opened up to somebody and that it felt like a burden was lifted off his shoulders. I am not new to the feeling anymore. When my story was released a heavy load was lifted off me. He is a humble survivor, and certainly seemed to have the potential to find success in the entertainment world. He already made his mark by writing a book with one of the most powerful titles "Attitude of Gratitude."

This wise young man got a glimpse of my story and saw my strength despite all the vulnerabilities. Most of the inspiration through the journey came to me from total strangers. Overtime we learn which hand to shake and which hand to hold.

Sadly, quite often we choose to be strangers and miss opportunities. Derris texted me a few days later! "Teera you showed me the way to be happy again. I am grateful."

Derris asked if I could video tape him sing a song he wrote. It was my first-time recording, but it came out pretty good. We were taping by the Corner Bakery Cafe on 8th and Figueroa in downtown Los Angeles.

The security officer might have heard the loud passionate voice, when he came by and asked us to leave, that is putting it mildly. I had a feeling it was probably not the place for Derris to sing his heart out from the moment he started. I was quite nervous, but he confidently finished singing the song.

He had two gifts for me. One of his paintings is called TOPICAL HAZE with a beautiful note written on the back, signed by Derris Nile on the 17th August 2018. He also took out the cross he wore around his neck, gave it to me and said "Teera, you need more protection now than me. It was an aww moment I will never forget. We had our picture taken by the water fountain at the Grand Hope park. While walking he looked deep into my eyes and said "don't throw the leftover food or drinks" leave it for the homeless and pointed out the places I should be leaving them and encouraged me to eat healthy. I noticed he fed Phoenix only healthy food.

The book "Attitude of Gratitude" written by Derris Nile is available on Amazon. Please! buy the book to support this brilliant, humble, caring, grateful young man. A messenger. It is hard to imagine a young man coming from a broken family had the capacity to write a book with the powerful title, having only his partner Phoenix by his side. Derris Nile certainly is a shining star brightening the world one day at a time.

"One voice can change the world" said Obama.

Derris' father kept telling him over and over that 'he would never amount to anything'. I saw a brilliant compassionate young man who has done way more than anyone I know, through stumbling stones that blocked his way. When I think of Derris, the following line comes to my mind from the famous song 'blowing in the wind", 'How many roads must a man walk down before you can call him a man'?

As the time passed by, I am amazed when I recall how Derris turned around and asked me what I was ordering, as if we knew each other and were in line together. Within two days I met two strangers who made a permanent mark on me.

***

42

SAMUEL – STANDING TALL

I took a walk by the lake several times, hoping to see Samuel for over a month almost every day and came to the conclusion, he might have found work. I kept telling myself somebody ought to tell him to share his story, which would be an eye opener wishing and hoping to see him on channel "OWN", to remind the dangers to those who still text and drive. I believe that there is a pretty good chance I might see him in the Oprah show one of these days.

One fine afternoon I was walking by the lake and passed a young man sitting in the same spot I met Samuel. I turned around and asked if he had seen a gentleman in a wheelchair with a broken leg. Amazingly he knew of Samuel and was very impressed with his uplifting positive attitude. He said his name is Darrell. I gave my phone number to him and asked him to have Samuel call me.

The next day Samuel called. I met him by the lake and gave him the printout of the article I wrote about him. However, I had left the last page while rushing to meet him. I promised to bring it to him the next time. He said he is excited to read my memoir and will have his son order it from Amazon.

I called him the following day and asked if he could meet me by the lake. He said he would be happy to come by my office instead. I took the opportunity to put a copy of my memoir in an envelope along with the last page of the article. I suggested he share his story with Oprah! As she makes it her call to send a message of the dangers of texting and driving with the hope that his story might be an eye-opener for those who still text and drive. There are many similar stories. We need to continue telling every tale with the hope of making a positive difference in the world and make the world a better place perhaps for generations. I encouraged him to write his many more compelling stories.

Samuel smiled when he opened the envelope and saw a copy of the memoir, then stood up instantly with a shining smile and thanked me. I was amazed to watch this handsome man standing tall on one leg. He said he might take a part time job as a driver soon and added that he is ready to write his stories and took off on his electric wheelchair with a wide smile on his face.

I am so glad; I did not give up looking for him. We bumped into each other a few times since then. Recently I walked by the lake hoping to meet him and give him a copy of the "EYE OPENER "article I wrote about Homelessness in LA. I walked around and sat down on a bench for a while hoping he would come by, but he did not.

I was on my way out of the park when I saw Samuel, this time on crutches, all dressed up. His bright smile made him look very attractive. He said he was on his way to teach a Bible class. I handed him the article and he was excited to read and share it with his students.

I am wishing and hoping to see Samuel on Oprah show soon.

***

43

STEVE – TILL LOVE COMES

I met another young artist with a different story. Steve ran away from home when he was a teenager. His father kept telling him he would never amount to anything, and one day attempted to strangle him to death out of jealousy. He is very angry with his alcoholic mom because she did not defend him and chose to stay with his abusive father. He said his mom is still very beautiful and looks like an actress! His father is possessive of his mom and did not want to share her with the two sons. He came to LA to follow his dream to be an actor, and a producer.

He told me he was gay and looking for love and hoping to find a partner to share his life soon. He turned 40 recently and wondered if he would find his soul mate. He is also a brilliant writer, singer, song writer and more. A young man with a heart of Gold, smart, spontaneous, who loves to have fun. I remembered a line Rick wrote "Life begins at 40" in one of his articles and passed it to him to give him hope, so he would stop looking for love and wait patiently for love to find him.

Steve reminds me of Patrick Lawrence, my ex-husband who keeps coming to my mind. He would have made a great public speaker! Come to think of it, he too came from a privileged family. His father was an overseer for the Ceylon Railway and retired with a grand pension for life. His older brother was a high rank officer in the Sri Lankan air force, sister, younger brothers, and cousins were all well-educated. Doctors, lawyers, Army commanders, the list can go on and on.

He was a genius who lived a troubled life. If someone who mattered to him and saw his brilliant intellect and understood him and his ability, he would have done great! Even change the world for the better. I saw his potential! I watched him read several papers cover to cover. He spoke about global affairs intelligently. I often reminded him if he gets his act together, he had the capacity to rise to the highest level of any profession. but sadly, he needed the approval of someone who really mattered to him. He certainly was a man with a brilliant intellect who turned to alcohol to numb the pain.

***

44

SERENITY – IN SEARCH OF AGAPE

Exactly one month later the 27th June, I met Frank. I heard a girl crying her heart out and saw her sitting on a staircase at the McArthur metro subway station. She raised her head and looked at me when I stopped and asked, "Why are you crying?" She did not answer. Then I asked, "Where are you going?" Without a beat she said, "wherever God takes me." I said, "That's me; I go with the flow, we certainly have something in common." Then she smiled. The train arrived at the station, and I said, "I have to go, "and got on the train.

Just as the doors were closing, she jumped in and sat on the floor close to where I stood and kept moving around her few belongings. She was restless. When I got off at the next station she too jumped off and walked by my side. I asked, "what is your name?" She said "Serenity", I replied, "wow, that's a beautiful name." I added, "I wake up every morning saying the serenity prayer." I could not just walk away from this vulnerable sad girl. While walking with me she humbly said she was hungry.

We bought some lunch and sat down. She started crying again. It was quiet first, then she lost control, she wailed then sobbed in exhaustion. I sat by her patiently. When she calmed down, I asked if she had siblings? She said "Yes, 25." She was adopted by a Mexican family along with 25 orphans. Now she is 19 years old. Her boyfriend of 4 years died of a drug overdose two months ago. She was into drugs but stopped after his death. She said it was meth.

I said to myself, more places similar to Covenant House are a necessity, to start over; for the youth who end up in cruel streets/ surroundings in distress, or who have no parent figure to count on or a home they can go back to find solace.

Serenity is homeless. She revealed to me schizophrenia makes her react under pressure. My thoughts were one of these days she might react aggressively and unknowingly making authorities very likely to put the traumatized girl in jail. She needs understanding and mental help, certainly not punishment. Jails are overcrowded with mentally ill young people as they were judged wrongly and written off as criminals. I wonder what happened to her 25 siblings! I might be bumping into some of the strangers who might be her siblings.

I have had several confusing experiences with people suffering with various mental illnesses. I am not qualified to help them. I understand emotional imbalance because I have been there. My emotions get the best of me at times. Sometimes we all need help in that area; someone to understand regardless of who or where we are through the journey.

"The enormous need to recognize mental illness is vital. The early treatment saves lives," said a billboard in a bus that I rode. I didn't have the knowledge or capacity to understand them, until I was surprised by people reacting aggressively when least expected to something I said or the way I looked at them unintentionally triggering them to react in anger towards me. I later realized how these conditions make them lose control under enormous pressure. Now I am cautious.

Those incidents made me speak less and listen more and I vowed to stop talking unless it was of any value. How easy is this lesson once we grasp the new concept? "Listening is an act of LOVE. Unconditional love, what the Greeks describe as 'agape' is distinct from other kinds of love between people.

The reminder of her cry haunted me, like my cry many decades ago. I walked the desert and understood how sad and lonely she felt. Our circumstances were different, but the pain, the grief and sorrow that are the cause of her depression is the same. It is hard to comprehend how debilitating a bout of depression is unless you have gone through one yourself. It is a mind-warping spiral where your brain does not have the physical capacity to function properly. I cannot stop wondering how she became an orphan. Her parents must have treasured their baby to name her Serenity which perfectly suited her personality. Sweet girl' well mannered! I hope and pray she will soon find courage and strength to move forward.

Suddenly, I had a flashback. I remembered the card that sister Mary Rose from Covenant House had sent me many years ago and referred to earlier which I had used for my fundraisers in Sri Lanka.

"On the street I saw a girl cold and shivering in a thin dress with little hope of a decent meal, I became very angry and said to God, why don't you do something about it? For a while God said nothing. That night he replied quite suddenly. "I certainly did do something about it, I made you."

The Card was an epiphany moment for me. I gave Serenity the directions to the Covenant House.

At that point all I could do was feed her and show her a way.

The possibilities to get things done are endless if we give time of the day to understand those in need with a helping hand with love and compassion. There is always something we can do if we care enough. I recall Mother Teresa's famous words of compassion. "We cannot do great things on this earth; we can do little things with great love." That evening I put away Sister. Mary Rose's card with my important documents for safekeeping.

***

Dear Teens,

I kind of wish God could write you this note. I mean, I know you and I have never met, and I desperately need to reach you right now.

I'd love to know what God would say to you if He were in my position. I'd love to see what He would say to convince you to help the kids in my crisis shelter.

"I really need you to read this note," He probably would say. "Some of my favorite kids in the whole world need your help," I think He would say. "I think you're one person who would want to know about these kids, and help them."

God knows, I need your help right now! Last night, we packed 1,200 homeless and runaway kids into our shelter. And I'll see 1,200 more tonight!

Please. Could you help me feed, and clothe, and care for these kids? Please. The need is urgent.

Thank you for helping, if you can.

In God's love,
Sister Mary Rose McGeady
President of Covenant House

COVENANT HOUSE

WHO AM I TO JUDGE

45
BARBARA – GYM IS HOME

On the 15th July I saw my new friend Barbara whom I met at the gym about a year ago. I had not seen her for the last two to three months. I told her of my concerns about the homeless and that I was writing an article to be published as the recent discoveries about the homeless in LA disturbed me tremendously. She surprised me by revealing that she has been homeless for the last 5 years. An English lady who was born and raised here. She said all I got was a glimpse of the problem. She experiences hopelessness because she lives among them and still hoping to live in a home again soon even though it seems farfetched after 5 years on the streets. She turned 79 on the 1st of August 2018.

She comes to the gym to shower and store her luggage during the day. She goes back and forth in the subway train at night and gets off to have breakfast in a small place that opens very early in the morning. Barbara revealed to me most of the homeless population is African American and added, "take my word for it, I have seen it all, not just a thing or two."

She criticized former president Obama and Oprah for not taking care of their people. She says both should go back to Africa where they belong. She complained about Oprah opening a school in Africa and buying a luxury car for her father's birthday. I attempted to reason with her by saying she bought the luxury car to honour her father, but I noticed she drove an ordinary car when she took a road trip with Gayle King. But Barbara has made up her mind and my words go deaf in her ears.

The drastic weather patterns even in LA; frequent heat waves and colder winters are not on their side either. All the unimaginable odds of survival are against them. The magnitude of the problem sounded like an impossible task to be accomplished. She revealed she was afraid to tell me she was homeless in the belief that I might not want to talk with her anymore. I understand as this is not uncommon in society. She is so grateful I decided to write about it and hugged me on her way out lovingly and gifted me a tiny stuffed dog with a tag written 'LOVE' I was in AWE! The hug and the gift spoke a thousand words of gratitude for a simple gesture. I promised to bring her a copy of the article.

During the time, my children and I lived in separation at the mercy of others as I did not have a place to call our home, my humble plea from God was granted graciously. We have been saved and it is our turn to save others. I write my heart out of deep love and reach out to God on behalf of those in need of a helping hand. The great church leader Andrew Murray once said. "Your heart is your world, and your world is your heart, and this is the place God works in your lives"

I met Barbara a week later, the 25th for lunch as planned and gave her a copy of the article. She got good news to share with me. She revealed the article to a lady friend and the lady graciously offered her the hospitality of her home. She was so excited when she had the lady speak to me on the phone. She said it would cost about $12 for the train fare to get to her place. I was so glad I had the opportunity to give Barbara the train fare. Barbara gave me her new phone number and said, 'I want to promote your book, on her way to the train with a shining smile. She kept waving at me while the train moved at a slow pace. I hoped and prayed that she will never have to be homeless again. Her attitude of gratitude for a small act of love uplifted my spirits and brought me pure joy, for I saw something and did something about it which opened a door for her.

**

46
MARCUS – UNRECOGNIZED OPPORTUNITY

It was 14th October, the day I learned there are homeless Uber Drivers too. You never know until you give them the time of day. Uber driver Marcus dropped me at the Union Station homeless shelter in Pasadena. I would never have imagined there is a homeless shelter in Pasadena called Union Station. I was supposed to join Pastor Millason Dailey and the volunteers from Calvary church to feed the homeless. I waited at the Union Station, Los Angeles when I was informed, I was at the wrong place. To avoid further delay I called Uber and the driver Marcus knew a faster way to the Union station homeless shelter.

"An inconvenience is an unrecognized opportunity said Confucius. If I did not have to take the Uber that evening and listened to Marcus, I would never have imagined there are homeless Uber drivers as well

I was late but made it in time to give a helping hand to the servers!

Marcus opened up to me and spoke nonstop about his struggle to survive. He was born and raised here in LA by loving parents. Then they moved to another state. When he lost his job, his loving grandmother invited him to stay in her house with her, but shortly she passed away and he became homeless.

Marcus is hoping to pay off the car Uber organization provided for him which has given him a second chance to get his life back in order. He works most of the day and is determined to make the best of the opportunity. Marcus sleeps at an abandoned house to get a few hours of sleep. I appreciate the Uber service very much, but the appreciation turned to gratitude for their service focused on the wellbeing of many also by providing environment friendly vehicles to the drivers who cannot afford to buy a car.

As time went by, I came to the realization that wherever there is a problem to be solved, there are creative people like those at Uber imagining a solution. I cannot think of a world without them.

Amazingly one leads to another. The abandoned house that Marcus sleeps in reminded me of the homeless young brilliant artist named Derris I met in Santa Monica.

I had met two young men that sleep in abandoned houses and wonder why there are abandoned houses in the City of Angels while there are so many homeless people looking for shelter.

There was nothing strange about the homeless strangers that crossed my path unexpectedly. These encounters compel me to write and share in the hope of making a positive difference in the world. Let this be a newsworthy "eye opener" for the news media. It is vital we act justly; be merciful and humbly pray for justice and liberty for all.

Let us feed one at a time, save one at a time; shelter one at a time, comfort one at a time. Hope begins with only one.

***

47

DAVE PELZER – MOVING FORWARD

Many years ago, I found a book on the sidewalk by a trash container which was written by Dave Pelzer titled "Moving forward" with the sub– title "Taking the lead in your life." After reading it, I purchased three more of his books. His mother brutally tortured and tormented Dave. He kept the family secret until the school nurse saw his nasty bruises. However, he endured the pain. He shows you how to let go of the past. He lives life to its fullest while maintaining dignity, self-esteem, and beliefs to make a positive difference in the world. His mother intimidated him to the extent that the fear that paralyzed him made him silent.

I have come to realize, it is better for a child to have one stable caring parent figure than two self-absorbed, self-centred, mentally disturbed parents.

***

48

PATRICK – SONG OF DEFIANCE

December 9th, I met a gentleman named Patrick who approached me at the Union Station. He was sitting in the opposite compartment. I saw he had a guitar with him.

When I got off at Union Station, he came to me and said, "You look happy." I smiled at him and said, "thank you" and asked if he makes music. He said yes "God gives gifts with hiccups." He added that he was hiding in the house because of the looks he gets from people as he cannot control his embarrassing hiccups. But that morning he said to himself, "Fuck everybody I am getting out of my shell."

It reminded me of the line, "You may be given a cactus, but you don't have to sit on it."

I told Patrick about my co-author Patrick and gave him my card. He said, "maybe one of these days we could have coffee." I agreed.

Patrick with the guitar reminded me of my friend Araceli I met a few years ago. We didn't know each other, however she came across my memoir, read it within two days and she said to me, "Teera, I love the way your story is written" You said "fuck everybody" when you put the book out there. She added our cultures are so similar. Overtime we became good friends and Araceli graciously helps me with my edits whenever I need help.

***

49
JULIE – UNCERTAIN DESTINY

On the 22nd June 2019 while waiting by the 'Crepe cafe' in Union station to pick a snack, I saw a newsletter left on the empty table next to me. I glanced at it and noticed that it was about a place called "Refresh spot" community-driven project that provides the skid row services. A spot open 24/7 includes a safe program which is designed to create added safety for guests and visitors near and around the skid row. I picked it up hoping to read more about the place, left it on the table and as soon as I sat down a lady passing by approached me. She asked me if I am from India or Sri Lanka and that she knows a Sri Lankan gentleman named Sumane who works in a prestigious hotel in San Diego. I realized she was homeless when I noticed the luggage she was pushing forward. I invited her to sit with me. She spoke nonstop about her struggles; she once was wealthy and became homeless due to unavoidable circumstances due to many sad tales. The skid row has taken a heavy toll on her face. Behind the wrinkles I saw someone who was once a beauty.

She noticed the newsletter on the table and said" Oh! This is the place I need to go." Then she wrote many phone numbers and addresses on the flyer and asked me humbly to contact them. Her beautiful writing was very clear. She told me her name is Julie and was born on 1st December 1944. Her birthdate reminded me of Barbara who turned 80 on the 1st August 2018. I gave her my card and revealed to her about my memoir. She wrote an address and said I should mail a couple of books to that address. She has a compelling story to tell, but she would not out of fear for her life she said to me. A young man who helps those on skid row got her the directions to the "Refresh spot' in Downtown Los Angeles.

When I called her son, he answered the phone in one ring, as if he were waiting for the call. He sounded so worried when he spoke to me with a heavy heart. He asked me to pass a message to her if I bump into her again. He can afford to settle her in a good home as he recently came into some settlement of a case that was pending for a long time. He said to me she has been giving his phone number to many strangers to call him, but she would not call him and told me she is mentally ill. My thoughts were having to survive in the cruel streets can drive anyone insane.

I called her brother as requested to let him know that she is doing alright. He was very thankful I passed the message.

***

50

BARBARA – BLURRED VISION

Barbara was on the road again. I bumped into her on the 12th February 2019. She said she prefers the road more than being stuck in a house. The subway train and fitness centre have become a sanctuary for her, along with many homeless people. She told me she had no energy to workout. After listening to Barbara, I did not feel bad about keeping my membership even though I hardly get to make time to work out, as someone like Barbara got a place to shower to clean up and rest a while.

She once again complained about the homeless population of African American community. I understood her concerns as she lives among them and sees their world more than beyond imagination. However, I could not resist and stay put anymore as she kept repeating that "they must go back to Africa, where they belong" with a smirk on her face. Her words disturbed me tremendously. After a pause I said "Barbara, their ancestors were bought for slavery and generations are born and raised here". Her specific statement was another eye opener that made me want to find the root cause of the problem way beneath the surface that creates unrest, division, and destruction in the society. Why and what triggered most of them to give up that easy.

I read that four centuries ago their ancestors were stolen from their country, enslaved. They were forced to do hard labour in farms. "Hardworking farmers should be the first to enjoy the fruits of their labour!"

People sometimes work overtime to outcast and to do terrible things to break the human spirit. Their ancestors were broken many times, in many ways. Small minds belittle others. We need to get into the habit of getting along. It is vital we practice understanding. Resentment and animosity towards each other are a waste of time. When we understand why people are the way they are, forgiveness comes easy.

My response made Barbara very angry. I certainly pushed a wrong button that threw her off balance. I just had to set the record straight and give her something to think about. More like when children behave badly Americans say, "go to your room and think about it." She kept shouting at me and said you and Patrick should stop writing immediately. The revelation came to me the moment she said to 'STOP WRITING' I slowly picked my backpack and walked away to avoid her as the lash outs got louder. I understood her frustrations, but I had to let her know I am not in agreement with her statement that people should go to where they belong. Vengeance is often a product of pride that destroys the peace. If someone hurts us, usually the instinct is a burning desire to "hit back" and "get even".

We may not realize it, but almost everyone has been subjected to discrimination for some ridiculous reason sometime or the other. Then again there are times we discriminate ourselves and blame others. The unmerited condemnation contaminates the world. Nature is not colour blind and does not discriminate Black or While. The colour of the skin one is born with should not be the way to judge one's character. Some are born different. Nobody is spared. Parents, children, friends, the list go on and on. It is something we all have in common that we can all identify with our experiences. Life is wonderful if we know how to live. True happiness comes when we overcome selfishness and avoid judgement. Egotistical hate blurs the vision and creates division.

***

51
BRIAN – RICHNESS OF DIVERSITY

There will always be disappointments and disagreements in life. The choice is whether we choose to overlook those faults in love or allow anger to rule our hearts. This incident also brought back the memories of a young man who committed suicide several years ago who was born and raised in California. I changed his name to Brian for the sake of privacy of his family. I knew him to be a charismatic, handsome young man when he was 19 years of age. We lost touch since he got married and met two decades later during the time, he was contemplating suicide. He was told over and over that he does not belong in the U.S. and should go back to Africa where he belonged.

Eventually, the negative words spoken over and over to him took a heavy toll on his mental health. One morning he took a gun out of his precious gun collection, sat on his living room sofa, and shot himself to death.

The day Barack Obama became president of the United States was a very exciting day. Brian came to my mind while I stayed glued to the television with amazement of that magical moment. I was sad he did not live to witness the victorious accomplishment of the brilliant African American gentleman who made history.

Barbara and I used to enjoy our conversations. In fact, she revealed some of her life stories to me. She wanted to write her compelling stories, but it is not that easy to write when one is homeless. She did not reveal to me she was homeless because of the fear of discrimination until I told her of my concerns of the homeless in L.A. I understand where she comes from and her point as she sees so much day in and day out. One can easily lose one's mind having to survive in the skid row. Our actions and conduct will have a greater impact on the people we move with than our words ever will. The Universe certainly has a way of connecting people in our lives for a reason, even the negative people. They open our eyes so we do not withhold things we can do to make the world a better place hopefully for generations to come.

Ambien Manufactures once issued a tweet, a brilliant line. "Racism is not a side effect of sleep medicine." Teachable words, to shut the loudmouth, blamed the medicine for the unfiltered discriminating words spoken towards African Americans.

Several years ago, a bunch of infuriated African American men misplaced their anger on innocent people to retaliate against the police brutality on a young man named Rodney King. Eventually Rodney King was approached to appease the situation. He calmly pleaded with smooth words of peace to stop the violence.

Just one line said it all. "Can we all get along?"

Yes, why can't we get along? Live simply and let others simply live in peace. The richness of diversity is the road to happiness. It is so simple, why complicate with harsh words in judgement?

***

52
TEERA – DARKNESS TO LIGHT

Discrimination comes in many forms, racial, gender, sexual orientation among many including simply those due to what life dishes out to people and I am an example of the latter.

In the movie "Time to Kill" Samuel Jackson (father) seeking justice for his little girl, put his life online. Some break the law, and some are broken by the law. The powerful message moved the world.

My father never got the chance to seek justice for his girl. He put the word out there hoping someone, anyone, that would listen, and news travels fast in the small town. Sadly, once the word got out, I was the one who got discriminated against and carried the burden as no one wanted to hear my side of the story. Discrimination leads to ugly rumours, maliciously ruin lives unjustly and the innocent suffer in silence.

After the tragedy I was discriminated against as an unlucky widow. The permanent scar made me discriminate myself. I recall one of my relatives bluntly told me to stay behind the curtain during her daughter's wedding. She told me I should not be seen by the bride when she walks in because I would bring bad luck to the bride. My brokenness made me accept the place I was put in humbly, but sadly. The permanent scar already made me feel ugly, less than human. The insensitive comment confirmed my feeling of inadequacy. I was marginalized for no fault of mine by the superstition carried on without any concern about my feelings.

Most beautiful people in the world are discriminated against because some are eager to marginalize fellow human beings. Ego! The superiority complex I believe is a mental illness. Holding on to grudges with Hate is the road to unhappiness that creates hell on earth. As a child I felt less than some because of the colour of my skin. It was a fact that light skinned girls were considered beautiful. However even through the daily drain of being in the minority, I found joy in given freedom by doing my sport activities.

Our story begins at home. We often develop inferiority complex and stumble through life feeling insecure, a lack of self-confidence and a sense of impending failure. Over time I learned beauty and colour are only skin deep.

***

53
DESMOND TUTU – GOD'S RESPONSE

A very beautiful inspirational story worthy of sharing was related by Rev. Desmond Tutu in a BBC program. He said when one day he and his mother were walking down the street a tall white man dressed in a black suit came towards them. This was in the days of apartheid in South Africa when a black person and a white person met on a footpath, the black person was expected to step into the gutter and allow the white person to pass and nod their head as a gesture of respect. But this day before the young Tutu and his mother could step off the sidewalk the white man stepped off the sidewalk and as they passed, he tipped his hat in a gesture of respect to her. The white man was Trevor Huddleston who stepped off the sidewalk because he was a man of God. Tutu said he found his calling when she told him that he was an Anglican priest. Hudson later became a mentor to Desmond Tutu and inculcated in him a commitment to the equality of all human beings as they are all created in the God's image. A key driver in Tutu's opposition to apartheid.

My prayer is that we can all strive to be people of God who are willing to step off the sidewalk and tip our hats to our sisters and brothers, particularly those marginalized from the society.

***

FINAL THOUGHTS

In the end, I have many questions about the homeless.

They must have a solid reason to suffer the consequences on the cruel streets. Could it be the misunderstood intentions, and the hostility on both sides?

Mother Teresa said, "We think sometimes that poverty is only being hungry, naked and homeless. Being unwanted, unloved and uncared for, is the greatest poverty."

Success Stories from the Frontlines

On the 27th June 2019, I attended an event organized by 'EVERY ONE IN' and listened to many victory stories of the homeless given a second chance to live a life that matters, by a caring bunch of people.

It was a very uplifting experience to listen to how ordinary people do extraordinary deeds, politics apart to make a positive difference in fellow human beings.

It has been 5+years since my memoir was published.

It was a mountain top experience, and there was work down below lined up for me. I had no choice, but to get out of my comfort zone, and look for places where I could breathe easy to find serenity. At times I walked aimlessly. In amazement I learned you are somebody's miracle. The answers I was searching came in the foam of many strangers who needed someone to listen. I have told my story and given my time to listen to their tales with love.

The God of the universe has a spectacular, anonymous way to let you know you survive for a higher purpose to experience the joy of putting others first. The highest worship is giving of yourself unselfishly. Never underestimate the power of loving humanity.

NONE OF US ARE WELL UNLESS ALL OF US ARE WELL. SACRIFICIAL LOVE IS THE WAY!

***

ANNEX

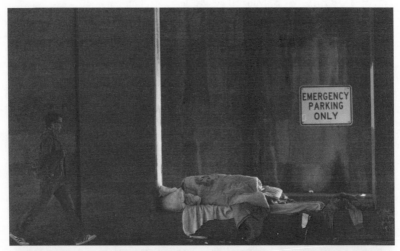

ANNEX

EXCERPTS OF PRESS REPORTS ON THE HOMELESS

NEW YORK TIMES, Marie Tae McDermott, Jan. 22, 2020
How Do People Become Homeless?
People who have experienced homelessness share their stories.

Karla Garcia
Karla lived in her van with her family throughout high school. She later received a full scholarship to attend U.C. Berkeley.

My father was a carpenter and my mother was an aide at a school library. During the Great Recession, my father was unable to find work and my mother's hours were cut. They could no longer afford their mortgage. We had to sell most of our things to keep the power on for as long as possible. We lost power, heat and water, and in the end, we were all sleeping in one mattress in an empty home we knew any minute would be repossessed. One afternoon, we came home to discover we were locked out of the house, and that's when we started living in our van. We went from having a normal life and stable housing, to being homeless. We didn't always have food, and sometimes my mother would have to choose between gas and food. My parents would take us to the park or to the beach to play all day. In a way, it was a time when I saw my parents and enjoyed them the most.

— Karla Garcia, 25, San Diego

Conor Kelly
Conor grew up in Palo Alto and as a result of substance addiction, he resorted to living on the streets for a year and a half.

I was so caught up in my addictions that a big part of me didn't want help. After first going to college, my partying got completely out of hand. I eventually was introduced to "harder" substances and became hopelessly addicted. I failed out and went through a series of rehabs to no avail. Eventually my degenerating behaviour shut me off from friends and family, and after getting kicked off the last couch, I went to the streets.

— Conor Kelly, 28, Santa Cruz

John Brady

John spent a year living on the streets because of depression and a lack of alternatives.

I have a master's degree in business and marketing. About a decade ago, I was the victim of a hate crime and did not get the treatment I needed. Instead, I self-medicated which led to some poor decisions, the loss of my business and ultimately homelessness. I spent just shy of a year on the streets of San Diego. I used to look at homelessness as a result of personal decisions. Now I see things much more clearly. The experience of being homeless is the most devastating of my life. I was suffering from major depressive disorder, anxiety and PTSD before I was on the street and those disorders only became worse while homeless. The one thing that kept me alive was the leadership of the Voices of Our City Choir and their belief in me.

— John Brady, 54, San Diego

Ethan Ward

Ethan used his college campus's facilities while living out of his car.

I was enrolled full time at Los Angeles City College and living solely off financial aid because my priority was finishing school as quickly as possible. Rent increased at my building and I had to choose between spending all my aid money on rent and not having money for anything else or living in my car. I chose to live in my car for a year instead. I quickly realized how easy it is for someone to lose housing and how that can eventually lead to losing hope. It was a daily chore to remind myself that homelessness was a temporary situation.

— Ethan Ward, 37, Los Angeles.

A. AMERICA'S CITIES COULD HOUSE EVERYONE IF THEY CHOSE TO - OUR HOUSING CRISIS IS A SYMPTOM OF AMERICA'S WEALTH — AND ITS INDIFFERENCE *(By Binyamin Appelbaum - Member of the New York Times editorial board, May 15, 2020)*

Tonight, more than half a million Americans will sleep in public places because they lack private spaces. They will huddle in crowded New York City shelters, or pitch tents under highways in Washington, D.C., or curl up in the doorways of San Francisco office towers or dig holes in the high desert of northern Los Angeles County.

They are homeless, and their lives are falling apart. They struggle to stay healthy, to hold jobs, to preserve personal relationships, to maintain a sense of hope.

They are victims of America's wealth — and its indifference.

Homelessness in the United States is the most extreme manifestation of a broader housing crisis. Even in the fat years before the coronavirus plunged the economy into recession, millions of Americans struggled to pay the rent, particularly in prospering coastal cities.

The federal government could render homelessness rare, brief and nonrecurring. The cure for homelessness is housing, and, as it happens, the money is available: Congress could shift billions in annual federal subsidies from rich homeowners to people who don't have homes.

Instead, Americans have taken to treating homelessness as a sad fact of life, as if it were perfectly normal that many thousands of adults and children in the wealthiest nation on earth cannot afford a place to live. Collectively, we are choosing to avert our eyes from the people who sleep where we walk. We have decided to live with the fact that some of our fellow Americans will die on the streets.

"There's a cruelty here that I don't think I've seen," Leilani Farha, then the United Nations special rapporteur on adequate housing, said after a 2018 visit to Northern California.

"I've never seen anything like it, and I've done outreach on every continent," Louise Casey, who directed homeless policy for several British prime ministers, said after touring homeless encampments in San Francisco, Los Angeles and other American cities.

Those who do end up homeless are often those with additional burdens. They are disproportionately graduating from foster care or the prison system, victims of domestic abuse or discrimination, veterans, and people with mental and physical disabilities. Some end up on the street because of addictions; some develop addictions because they are on the street. Whatever problems they face, however, they are much more likely to become homeless in places without enough affordable housing.

Americans must decide whether we are willing to let elementary school students spend nights in guarded parking lots, like ones I saw proliferating across the Western United States. We must decide whether it's worth spending just a little of this nation's vast wealth to ensure that no 60-year-old woman needs to sleep on the same bench in downtown Santa Monica, Calif., night after night because, as she explained to me, it's relatively flat and easy for the police to see her from their cars. We must decide whether it's tolerable for people to live in tents on the scraps of green space along a highway in Washington, D.C., just a short walk from the block where the richest man in America combined two mansions to create the city's largest.

Addressing homelessness is within our power. The question is whether we are ready to act.

B. MOVING THE HOMELESS – COVID TIME. *(Doug Smith – Senior Writer, Los Angeles Times – Pulitzer Prize Winner, 22 June 2020).*

Hoping to prevent a surge of deadly coronavirus cases in the homeless community, Los Angeles officials have launched an effort to move an unprecedented 15,000 people out of overcrowded shelters and encampments and into hotel rooms.

It's a daunting goal, given that nearly 60,000 people live without permanent shelter in L.A. County, most of them sleeping in the streets each night. Getting every person into an emergency shelter or a hotel room is probably an impossible task.

But in recent weeks, city and county officials, guided by the Los Angeles Homeless Services Authority, settled on the smaller number of 15,000 because it accounts for the segment of the homeless population most likely to die on the streets — with or without the pandemic: those who are seniors and are medically fragile.

The state has set its own goal of leasing 15,000 hotel and motel rooms for homeless people. Moving quickly is critical. If the authority can secure 15,000 rooms and fill them, it could prevent 1,400 hospitalizations and 350 deaths, according to an analysis by Randall Kuhn, the UCLA researcher who led a study on how many homeless people could die from COVID-19.

Unlike in other cities and counties, where opposition from elected officials, hotel owners and the public have stifled plans for homeless housing, all the major players in Los Angeles are on board. The Hotel Assn. of Los Angeles, contacted by the county for help, has turned over a list of 270 hotels with 25,000 rooms whose owners are willing to participate. Funding for the $190-million effort is largely secure through a Federal Emergency Management Agency commitment to reimburse 75% of the per-room cost. But timing is another matter.

C. HE DIED SUNDAY ON A WEST L.A. SIDEWALK. HE WAS HOMELESS. HE IS PART OF AN EPIDEMIC. (*C. Steve Lopez, Pulitzer Prize Winner, Los Angeles Times, September 4, 2019*)

The balding, middle-aged man was face down on a flattened piece of cardboard, arms at his side, a small pool of blood near his mouth. He wore blue jeans, his feet were bare, and headset buds were still in his ears.

Two LAPD officers who responded to the emergency call from a passer-by had pitched a white pop-up tent around the body, which lay on the sidewalk of Massachusetts Avenue between Sepulveda Boulevard and the 405 Freeway in West Los Angeles.

It was Sunday morning, the middle of Labor Day weekend, three-quarters of the way into a year in which deaths of homeless people in Los Angeles County are on a record-setting pace to top 1,000, according to preliminary numbers from the county coroner.

"I hope this will be another wake-up call that urgency is the order of the day," said County Supervisor Mark Ridley-Thomas, who called it incomprehensible and unacceptable that dying on the streets has become routine.

On average, nearly three homeless people are dying daily in the county, nearly double the rate of deaths by homicide. Illness, addiction, accidents, suicide, and the ravages of being unsheltered are among the primary causes of death.

The average age of the first 666 homeless people who died in L.A. County as of Aug. 25 was 51, well below the county's average life expectancy of roughly 80. Homeless people are dying on sidewalks, along riverbeds, and in tents, parks, shelters, vehicles, motels and hospitals. You can call it a travesty. An emergency. A call to action. It is all those things.

Bodies are being found in virtually every corner of the county, a grim consequence of the intensifying epidemic of homelessness. In 2012, 407 homeless people died in L.A. County. The number has gone up sharply every year, to last year's record high of 921.

This year, the toll hit 525 in just the first six months — 88 more than over the same period a year earlier — and the pace has been steady since then.

New York City has roughly the same number of homeless people as Los Angeles County, but has moved tens of thousands of them into shelters. Despite much harsher weather, New York recorded 292 homeless deaths in 2018, fewer than one-third the Los Angeles total.

The coroner's reports, filled with clinical language and dispassionate narratives, are ghostly sketches of social disorder, poverty, violence, addiction, and isolation. They speak to a breakdown that extends beyond homelessness and reaches into our economy, our schools, our criminal justice, and healthcare systems.

In a region of abundant wealth and world-class hospitals, people die penniless, they die in pain, they die alone.

D. NEW YORK TIMES LETTERS TO THE EDITOR

1. To the Editor:
It is unconscionable in the richest country in the world that there are millions of homeless people, including more than 114,000 homeless school-age children in New York City alone. Perhaps those living in mansions could be persuaded to set an example and spend some of their billions to build housing for the homeless. What a heart-warming story that would be. - Carol Delaney, Providence, R.I

2. To the Editor:
It was so poignant to consider that these were just two of the 114,000 stories, and the others are untold. It was crushing to hear about the lengths that these kids go to overcome the obstacles to an education they face. And an education is what will lift these kids out of homelessness and poverty and offer a chance for a better life. - Hannah Ritchey, New York.

***

ACKNOWLEDEMENTS

I wish to express my profound gratitude to Dr. Nandasiri (Nandi) Jasentuliyana for his encouragement and guidance. I am indebted to him for volunteering his valuable time to edit this publication and provide me with the confidence that my experiences narrated within these covers are worthy of publication. It is an honor and a great privilege to bring you, along with Nandi, the stories of those experiences woven around the encounters with the strangers who crossed my path.

I am deeply grateful to his lovely wife, Shanthi, for her patience and sacrifice during the period Nandi was glued to this project.

I want to compliment Manjula Kumara Gamage for his outstanding work designing an exceptionally attractive cover, formatting the book, and seeing through its printing process.

I am obliged to Neil and Upamali for reading my memoir and taking the initiative to pass it on to Nandi, which paved the way to the collaboration with Nandi in this sequel, which turned out to be a walk in the park.

I am grateful to Diana for reading my initial drafts and providing me with constructive criticism. Those comments surprised me as they came from a teenager, but the tenacity and honesty displayed in those valuable comments were immeasurable.

I am most appreciative of Andrea for her encouragement, and input in sharing the stories and the sentiments about the homelessness in the City of Angeles while I stayed in her checkout counter, which immensely enriched this publication.

I CHERISH THE PLEASANT MEMORIES WITH SINCERE GRATITUDE TO ALL. - Teera